THE GREATEST
THING IN THE WORLD
and other addresses

HENRY DRUMMOND
1851–1897

Titles in Collins Greetings Booklets

A SHAKESPEARE ANTHOLOGY

THE RUBÁIYÁT OF OMAR KHÁYYAM

THE GREATEST THING IN THE WORLD

MY LADY OF THE CHIMNEY CORNER

THE ROADMENDER

A WORDSWORTH ANTHOLOGY

LYRICS FROM THE GILBERT AND SULLIVAN OPERAS

A BOOK OF DAILY READINGS

THE LIFE AND TEACHINGS OF CHRIST

AN OPEN AIR ANTHOLOGY

AS A MAN THINKETH

A DICKENS ANTHOLOGY

CHURCHILL: HIS WIT AND WISDOM

STREAMLINED THOUGHTS

THE GREATEST
THING IN THE WORLD
and other addresses

HENRY DRUMMOND

With an Introduction by
J. Y. SIMPSON

COLLINS
LONDON AND GLASGOW

GREETINGS BOOKS

GENERAL EDITOR: G. F. MAINE

Printed in Great Britain by
COLLINS CLEAR-TYPE PRESS

CONTENTS

CONTENTS

INTRODUCTION

HENRY DRUMMOND was born at Stirling on the 17th of August, 1851; he died at Tunbridge Wells on March 11th, 1897. Consequently his life, in the maturity of its powers, was lived through a most distinctive period—the last quarter of last century—when the full impact of the truth that was in Darwin was rapidly being felt far beyond the narrow scientific area of its first dominance, under the sledge-hammer blows of a Huxley or the more overwhelming torrent of the Spencerian philosophy. The noble if placid orthodoxy of the greater Victorian poets notwithstanding, a ferment was at work in the minds of many of the younger generation, which in some cases resolved itself into a struggle between loyalty to an old theology or to a new science that were felt to be incompatible with one another. Realising the basal correspondences and unity of the truth which could be reached along the various highways of Revelation, Henry Drummond, with an inherited love for, and broadly

developed interest in, Natural Science, strove
to convey to others those glimpses of a wider
outlook and flashes from a penetrative insight
that had cheered and illumined his own too
solitary path. To what extent he had met a
need of his generation may be gathered from
the fact that the British sales of one of his larger
works,—*Natural Law in the Spiritual World*—
reached something like 130,000 copies, whilst of
the addresses here published, that one which
gives title to the volume had in his lifetime a
circulation of 350,000 in booklet form. His
writings provoked criticism in many undiscern-
ing quarters, but it is noteworthy that one of
the most distinguished of his critics, long years
after, made public avowal of how completely
he had failed to gauge the need for, or estimate
the value of, the kind of work, viz., that on
the relations of scientific and religious thought,
done by Drummond. It is a need that has only
become more clamant with the passage of the
years.

Under the moulding influence of an ideal
home life, Henry Drummond passed by way of
Edinburgh University, which he entered at the
age of fifteen, into New College, Edinburgh,
although with no very clear idea as to how the

"call" to religious service which had led him thither, might eventually be responded to in his particular case. At no time, apparently, had he ever thought of the active ministry, and his interest in his scientific studies had never slackened. The natural bent of his mind towards preoccupation with the relations of scientific and religious thought was seen in the subjects that were selected by him for class or Debating Society essays during his student days, as e.g. the "Six Days of Creation"; "Was the Deluge Partial?"; "The Doctrine of Creation." Then, in the third winter of his theological studies, he was swept into the current of the great Mission conducted by Messrs. Moody and Sankey in Great Britain during 1873-1875. It was an experience in which he found himself, and in which men began to realise his extraordinary powers of expression and appeal. "There's nobody in the world like Drummond for interesting young men," Mr. Moody had said; "set him to talk to a lot of 'em, and he'll just crop 'em in in five minutes." The Mission ended, he returned after two years' absence to the class-room benches, and quietly resumed his student place as if nothing had happened. Yet very much had happened, for while in the midst of the Mission he could say that "underlying my scientific studies and everything else, there has been this one settled conviction all these years—that the only life which to me would seem at all worth living would be a life of evangelistic work," a fuller experience had shown him that "the great thing is to *live* rather than to *work*," and that the immediate business for him now was in quietness and confidence to prepare himself spiritually for what he had no doubt would be made clear as God's purpose in life for him.

Very soon his way became clear before him. In the autumn of 1877 he applied for the vacant lectureship on Natural Science in the Free Church College, Glasgow, and helped largely by a very commendatory testimonial from Sir Sir Archibald Geikie, whom he later accompanied on a geological expedition to the Rocky Mountains, was elected to the post. Yet even with this definite demanding work in hand, he could not neglect the gift of evangelism that was in him. "I want a quiet mission somewhere," he wrote, "entry immediate and self-contained." It was his artisan audiences in Possilpark, Glasgow, who first heard the addresses that were afterwards collected and published as *Natural Law in the Spiritual World*. When, as the result of his work, the mission at Possilpark was made into a full charge, Henry Drummond retired from that post, and an ordained minister was appointed in his place. On his return from Africa in the spring of 1884 his lectureship, to which he had been re-appointed year by year, was raised to the status of a Chair through the vision and generosity of Mr. James Stevenson of Hailie, and he, unruffled by the rapidly mounting sales of his now famous book and the growing requests of those who sought spiritual counsel from him, was unanimously elected to the post by the General Assembly of his Church. His inaugural lecture on "The Contribution of Science to Christianity," when published later, added greatly to his reputation.

The year 1885 is still remembered by an older generation as the commencement of the long and happy association of Henry Drummond with the student life of Edinburgh University. In the autumn of 1884 the student world of Great Britain was stirred by the news that Stanley Smith and C. T. Studd, two brilliant Cambridge athletes, had resolved, along with five of their college friends, to devote themselves to mission work in China. Previous to their departure, the two leaders paid a series of farewell visits to various other Universities, and made such a deep impression in Edinburgh that they were invited to return if possible, which they did, within two months' time. The results were so profoundly moving that the local leaders felt that the work must be continued. Now it happened that in between the two visits of the Cambridge volunteers, Professor Drummond had delivered the annual lecture to the Christian Medical Association of Edinburgh University, taking as his subject "The Contribution of Science to Christianity." After that evening, when over four hundred men were captured by his presentation of old truth in a new light, it was not difficult to know who should be invited to carry on the work. Most fortunately he accepted the invitation, and for ten years, until he was stricken by the illness which proved fatal, he addressed meetings of Edinburgh University students in the Oddfellows' Hall for from four to six Sundays every spring. Of those who assisted him most, probably least will ever be known. The earlier years were particularly memorable, for small deputations of the men, headed by a professor or lecturer, visited the other Scottish Universities in turn, where, at meetings recognised by the local teaching staff, Christian Associations were formed, and the religious life of the University quickened. The resulting Holiday Mission, carefully organised under Drummond's immediate supervision, took groups of students to other towns and villages, and it is noteworthy that he made it a rule on all these occasions that the student members of the deputations should, so far as they went beyond describing the Edinburgh work confine themselves merely to testifying to some truth that they had made their own by personal experience. In time news of the work reached far beyond Great Britain. As a result, on two occasions in the United States, in Australia, and on the Continent, Henry Drummond went by invitation from University to University and College to College, sometimes accompanied by a representative deputation of Edinburgh professors or students, proclaiming the truth as he had come to see it. There are those who still remember the thrill with which they first heard the outlines of the address on Love at a Northfield Conference, U.S.A., in the summer of 1887, although it had certainly been given some four years earlier at a mission station service in Central Africa.

To few men of science is it given to write with clarity and distinction. From an early period Henry Drummond had practised writing and in his later years became almost fastidious about phrasing and expression. In particular he would insist on the careful selection of adjectives, a part of speech which he considered to be especially determinative of the care that a writer put into his work. So it is not surprising to learn that the original Introduction to *The Ascent of Man*, his greatest book, was, after being set up in type, entirely re-written and reduced in length as the result of a friendly criticism, or that he had a large first edition of one of his booklets suppressed just before publication, because he discovered a faulty paragraph in it at the last moment,—"a knot in the porridge," as he put it. Some may recall his mot, " *A Nineteenth Century* article should be written at least three times, once in simplicity, once in profundity, and once to make the profundity appear simplicity." Even more strongly he wrote to a young friend in 1895, "For your humility read Frederick Harrison's article in the October number of *The Nineteenth Century* on Ruskin as a Master of English Prose. After reading it you will wonder, as I did, however any of us have the face to print a line."

Concerning his message, the addresses speak for themselves. They are as vital and constraining to-day as when he first delivered them. They gripped men; they changed lives, not for a day but for all time. "I continually meet men from the Edinburgh meetings, holding like limpets," he wrote in 1890, during his tour in Australia. And his influence abides. Enter the private office of the Chief Magistrate of the capital city of Scotland, and the first thing that catches your eye is an enlarged photograph of Henry Drummond, and it would not be difficult to name man after man at the top of his profession to-day who would admit that one of the greatest influences for good in his life under God was Henry Drummond. This man, with something of the cavalier about him,—the students most closely associated with him in his work invariably spoke of him as "The Prince,"—with his wonderful power of literary expression, fine distinction of mind, and above all that selfless redemptive note about his life which was its key-note, eludes all efforts at portrayal. But that which he was, which he had at heart, and which was continuously exemplified in his life, may be glimpsed anew and savingly realised by another generation through his words.

J. Y. SIMPSON.

THE GREATEST
THING IN THE WORLD

Though I speak with the tongues of men and of angels, and have not Love, I am become as sounding brass, or a tinkling cymbal. And though I have the gift of prophecy, and understand all mysteries, and all knowledge; and though I have all faith, so that I could remove mountains, and have not Love, I am nothing. And though I bestow all my goods to feed the poor, and though I give my body to be burned, and have not Love, it profiteth me nothing. Love suffereth long, and is kind; Love envieth not; Love vaunteth not itself, is not puffed up, doth not behave itself unseemly, seeketh not her own, is not easily provoked, thinketh no evil; Rejoiceth not in iniquity, but rejoiceth in the truth; Beareth all things, believeth all things, hopeth all things, endureth all things.

Love never faileth: but whether there be prophecies, they shall fail; whether there be tongues, they shall cease; whether there be knowledge, it shall vanish away. For we know in part, and we prophesy in part. But when that which is perfect is come, then that which is in part shall be done away. When I was a child, I spake as a child, I understood as a child, I thought as a child; but when I became a man, I put away childish things. For now we see through a glass, darkly; but then face to face: now I know in part; but then shall I know even as also I am known. And now abideth faith, hope, Love, these three; but the greatest of these is Love.—I Cor. 13.

THE GREATEST
THING IN THE WORLD

EVERY ONE has asked himself the great question of antiquity as of the modern world: What is the *summum bonum*—the supreme good? You have life before you. Once only you can live it. What is the noblest object of desire, the supreme gift to covet?

We have been accustomed to be told that the greatest thing in the religious world is Faith. That great word has been the key-note for centuries of the popular religion; and we have easily learned to look upon it as the greatest thing in the world. Well, we are wrong. If we have been told that, we may miss the mark. I have taken you, in the chapter which I have just read, to Christianity at its source; and there we have seen, "The greatest of these is love." It is not an over-sight. Paul was speaking of faith just a moment before. He says, "If I have all faith, so that I can remove mountains, and have not love, I am nothing." So far from forgetting, he deliberately con-

trasts them, "Now abideth Faith, Hope, Love,"
and without a moment's hesitation, the
decision falls, "The greatest of these is Love."

And it is not prejudice. A man is apt to
recommend to others his own strong point.
Love was not Paul's strong point. The observ-
ing student can detect a beautiful tenderness
growing and ripening all through his character
as Paul gets old; but the hand that wrote,
"The greatest of these is love," when we meet
it first, is stained with blood.

Nor is this letter to the Corinthians peculiar
in singling out love as the *summum bonum*. The
masterpieces of Christianity are agreed about it.
Peter says, "Above all things have fervent love
among yourselves." *Above all things*. And John
goes farther, "God is love." And you remember
the profound remark which Paul makes else-
where, "Love is the fulfilling of the law." Did
you ever think what he meant by that? In
those days men were working their passage to
Heaven by keeping the Ten Commandments,
and the hundred and ten other commandments
which they had manufactured out of them.
Christ said, I will show you a more simple
way. If you do one thing, you will do these
hundred and ten things, without ever thinking

about them. If you love, you will unconsciously
fulfil the whole law. And you can readily see
for yourselves how that must be so. Take any
of the commandments. "Thou shalt have no
other gods before Me." If a man love God, you
will not require to tell him that. Love is the
fulfilling of that law. "Take not His name in
vain." Would he ever dream of taking His
name in vain if he loved Him? "Remember
the Sabbath day to keep it holy." Would he not
be too glad to have one day in seven to dedicate
more exclusively to the object of his affection?
Love would fulfil all these laws regarding God.
And so, if he loved Man, you would never think
of telling him to honour his father and mother.
He could not do anything else. It would be
preposterous to tell him not to kill. You could
only insult him if you suggested that he should
not steal—how could he steal from those he
loved? It would be superfluous to beg him not
to bear false witness against his neighbour. If
he loved him it would be the last thing he
would do. And you would never dream of
urging him not to covet what his neighbours
had. He would rather they possessed it than
himself. In this way "Love is the fulfilling of
the law." It is the rule for fulfilling all rules,

the new commandment for keeping all the old commandments, Christ's one secret of the Christian life.

Now Paul had learned that; and in this noble eulogy he has given us the most wonderful and original account extant of the *summum bonum.* We may divide it into three parts. In the beginning of the short chapter, we have Love *contrasted*; in the heart of it, we have Love *analysed*; towards the end we have Love *defended* as the supreme gift.

The Contrast

Paul begins by contrasting Love with other things that men in those days thought much of. I shall not attempt to go over those things in detail. Their inferiority is already obvious.

He contrasts it with eloquence. And what a noble gift it is, the power of playing upon the souls and wills of men, and rousing them to lofty purposes and holy deeds. Paul says, "If I speak with the tongues of men and of angels, and have not love, I am become as sounding brass, or a tinkling cymbal." And we all know why. We have all felt the brazenness of words without emotion, the hollowness, the unaccountable unpersuasiveness, of eloquence behind which lies no Love.

He contrasts it with prophecy. He contrasts it with mysteries. He contrasts it with faith. He contrasts it with charity. Why is Love greater than faith? Because the end is greater than the means. And why is it greater than charity? Because the whole is greater than the part. Love is greater than faith, because the end is greater than the means. What is the use of having faith? It is to connect the soul with God. And what is the object of connecting man with God? That he may become like God. But God is Love. Hence Faith, the means, is in order to Love, the end. Love, therefore, obviously is greater than faith. It is greater than charity, again, because the whole is greater than a part. Charity is only a little bit of Love, one of the innumerable avenues of Love, and there may even be, and there is, a great deal of charity without Love. It is a very easy thing to toss a copper to a beggar in the street; it is generally an easier thing than not to do it. Yet Love is just as often in the withholding. We purchase relief from the sympathetic feelings roused by the spectacle of misery, at the copper's cost. It is too cheap—too cheap for us, and often too dear for the beggar. If we really loved him we would either do more for him, or less.

Then Paul contrasts it with sacrifice and martyrdom. And I beg the little band of would-be missionaries—and I have the honour to call some of you by this name for the first time—to remember that though you give your bodies to be burned, and have not Love, it profits nothing—nothing! You can take nothing greater to the heathen world than the impress and reflection of the Love of God upon your own character. That is the universal language. It will take you years to speak in Chinese, or in the dialects of India. From the day you land, that language of Love, understood by all, will be pouring forth its unconscious eloquence. It is the man who is the missionary, it is not his words. His character is his message. In the heart of Africa, among the great Lakes, I have come across black men and women who remembered the only white man they ever saw before—David Livingstone; and as you cross his footsteps in that dark continent, men's faces light up as they speak of the kind Doctor who passed there years ago. They could not understand him; but they felt the Love that beat in his heart. Take into your new sphere of labour, where you also mean to lay down your life, that simple charm, and your lifework must succeed. You can take nothing greater, you need take nothing less. It is not worth while going if you take anything less. You may take every accomplishment; you may be braced for every sacrifice; but if you give your body to be burned, and have not Love, it will profit you and the cause of Christ *nothing*.

The Analysis

After contrasting Love with these things, Paul in three verses, very short, gives us an amazing analysis of what this supreme thing is. I ask you to look at it. It is a compound thing, he tells us. It is like light. As you have seen a man of science take a beam of light and pass it through a crystal prism, as you have seen it come out on the other side of the prism broken up into its component colours—red, and blue, and yellow, and violet, and orange, and all the colours of the rainbow—so Paul passes this thing, Love, through the magnificent prism of his inspired intellect, and it comes out on the other side broken up into its elements. And in these few words we have what one might call the Spectrum of Love, the analysis of Love. Will you observe what its elements are? Will you notice that they have common names; that they are virtues which we hear about every day; that they are things which can be practised by every man in every place in life; and how, by a multitude of small things and ordinary virtues, the supreme thing, the *summum bonum*, is made up?

The Spectrum of Love has nine ingredients:

Patience	"Love suffereth long."
Kindness	"And is kind."
Generosity	"Love envieth not."
Humility	"Love vaunteth not itself, is not puffed up."
Courtesy	"Doth not behave itself unseemly."
Unselfishness	"Seeketh not her own."
Good Temper	"Is not easily provoked."
Guilelessness	"Thinketh no evil."

Sincerity "Rejoiceth not in iniquity,
but rejoiceth in the truth."

Patience; kindness; generosity; humility;
courtesy; unselfishness; good temper; guilelessness; sincerity—these make up the supreme
gift, the stature of the perfect man. You will
observe that all are in relation to men, in
relation to life, in relation to the known to-day
and the near to-morrow, and not to the
unknown eternity. We hear much of love to
God; Christ spoke much of love to man. We
make a great deal of peace with heaven; Christ
made much of peace on earth. Religion is not
a strange or added thing, but the inspiration
of the secular life, the breathing of an eternal
spirit through this temporal world. The
supreme thing, in short, is not a thing at all,
but the giving of a further finish to the multi-
tudinous words and acts which make up the
sum of every common day.

There is no time to do more than make a
passing note upon each of these ingredients.
Love is *Patience*. This is the normal attitude of
Love; Love passive, Love waiting to begin;
not in a hurry; calm; ready to do its work
when the summons comes but meantime

wearing the ornament of a meek and quiet spirit. Love suffers long; beareth all things; believeth all things; hopeth all things. For Love understands, and therefore waits.

Kindness. Love active. Have you ever noticed how much of Christ's life was spent in doing kind things—in *merely* doing kind things? Run over it with that in view, and you will find that He spent a great proportion of His time simply in making people happy, in doing good turns to people. There is only one thing greater than happiness in the world, and that is holiness; and it is not in our keeping; but what God *has* put in our power is the happiness of those about us, and that is largely to be secured by our being kind to them.

"The greatest thing," says some one, "a man can do for his Heavenly Father is to be kind to some of His other children." I wonder why it is that we are not all kinder than we are. How much the world needs it. How easily it is done. How instantaneously it acts. How infallibly it is remembered. How superabundantly it pays itself back—for there is no debtor in the world so honourable, so superbly honourable, as Love. "Love never faileth." Love is success, Love is happiness, Love is life.

"Love," I say with Browning, "is energy of Life."

"For life, with all it yields of joy and woe
  And hope and fear,
  Is just our chance o' the prize of learning
      love—
  How love might be, hath been indeed, and is."

Where Love is, God is. He that dwelleth in Love dwelleth in God. God is love. Therefore *love*. Without distinction, without calculation, without procrastination, love. Lavish it upon the poor, where it is very easy; especially upon the rich, who often need it most; most of all upon your equals, where it is very difficult, and for whom perhaps we each do least of all. There is a difference between *trying to please* and *giving pleasure*. Give pleasure. Lose no chance of giving pleasure. For that is the ceaseless and anonymous triumph of a truly loving spirit. "I will pass through this world but once. Any good thing therefore that I can do, or any kindness that I can show to any human being, let me do it now. Let me not defer it or neglect it, for I shall not pass this way again."

Generosity. "Love envieth not." This is Love

in competition with others. Whenever you attempt a good work you will find other men doing the same kind of work, and probably doing it better. Envy them not. Envy is a feeling of ill-will to those who are in the same line as ourselves, a spirit of covetousness and detraction. How little Christian work even is a protection against un-Christian feeling. That most despicable of all the unworthy moods which cloud a Christian's soul assuredly waits for us on the threshold of every work, unless we are fortified with this grace of magnanimity. Only one thing truly need the Christian envy, the large, rich, generous soul which " envieth not."

And then, after having learned all that, you have to learn this further thing, *Humility*— to put a seal upon your lips and forget what you have done. After you have been kind, after Love has stolen forth into the world and done its beautiful work, go back into the shade again and say nothing about it. Love hides even from itself. Love waives even self-satisfaction. " Love vaunteth not itself, is not puffed up."

The fifth ingredient is a somewhat strange one to find in this *summum bonum*: *Courtesy*.

This is Love in society, Love in relation to etiquette. "Love doth not behave itself unseemly." Politeness has been defined as love in trifles. Courtesy is said to be love in little things. And the one secret of politeness is to love. Love *cannot* behave itself unseemly. You can put the most untutored person into the highest society, and if they have a reservoir of love in their heart, they will not behave themselves unseemly. They simply cannot do it. Carlyle said of Robert Burns that there was no truer gentleman in Europe than the ploughman-poet. It was because he loved everything—the mouse, and the daisy, and all the things, great and small, that God had made. So with this simple passport he could mingle with any society, and enter courts and palaces from his little cottage on the banks of the Ayr. You know the meaning of the word "gentleman." It means a gentle man—a man who does things gently, with love. And that is the whole art and mystery of it. The gentle man cannot in the nature of things do an ungentle, an ungentlemanly thing. The ungentle soul, the inconsiderate, unsympathetic nature cannot do anything else. "Love doth no behave itself unseemly."

Unselfishness. "Love seeketh not her own."
Observe: Seeketh not even that which is her
own. In Britain the Englishman is devoted,
and rightly, to his rights. But there come
times when a man may exercise even the higher
right of giving up his rights. Yet Paul does
not summon us to give up our rights. Love
strikes much deeper. It would have us not
seek them at all, ignore them, eliminate the
personal element altogether from out calcula-
tions. It is not hard to give up our rights.
They are often external. The difficult thing is
to give up ourselves. The more difficult thing
still is not to seek things for ourselves at all.
After we have sought them, bought them,
won them, deserved them, we have taken the
cream off them for ourselves already. Little
cross then, perhaps, to give them up. But not
to seek them, to look every man not on his
own things, but on the things of others—*id
opus est.* "Seekest thou great things for thyself?" said the prophet; "*seek them not.*" Why?
Because there is no greatness in *things*. Things
cannot be great. The only greatness is unselfish
love. Even self-denial in itself is nothing, is
almost a mistake. Only a great purpose or a
mightier love can justify the waste. It is more

difficult, I have said, not to seek our own at all, than, having sought it, to give it up. I must take that back. It is only true of a partly selfish heart. Nothing is a hardship to Love, and nothing is hard. I believe that Christ's yoke is easy. Christ's "yoke" is just His way of taking life. And I believe it is an easier way than any other. I believe it is a happier way than any other. The most obvious lesson in Christ's teaching is that there is no happiness in having and getting anything, but only in giving. I repeat, *there is no happiness in having, or in getting, but only in giving.* And half the world is on the wrong scent in the pursuit of happiness. They think it consists in having and getting, and in being served by others. It consists in giving and serving others. He that would be great among you, said Christ, let him serve. He that would be happy, let him remember that there is but one way—it is more blessed, it is more happy, to give than to receive.

The next ingredient is a very remarkable one: *Good Temper.* "Love is not easily provoked." Nothing could be more striking than to find this here. We are inclined to look upon bad temper as a very harmless weakness. We

speak of it as a mere infirmity of nature, a
family failing, a matter of temperament, not
a thing to take into very serious account in
estimating a man's character. And yet here,
right in the heart of this analysis of love, it
finds a place; and the Bible again and again
returns to condemn it as one of the most
destructive elements in human nature.

The peculiarity of ill temper is that it is the
vice of the virtuous. It is often the one blot
on an otherwise noble character. You know
men who are all but perfect, and women who
would be entirely perfect, but for an easily
ruffled, quick-tempered, or "touchy" disposition. This compatability of ill temper with
high moral character is one of the strangest
and saddest problems of ethics. The truth is
there are two great classes of sins—sins of the
Body, and sins of the *Disposition*. The Prodigal
Son may be taken as a type of the first, the
Elder Brother of the second. Now society has
no doubt whatever as to which of these is the
worse. Its brands falls, without a challenge,
upon the Prodigal. But are we right? We have
no balance to weigh one another's sins, and
coarser and finer are but human words ; but
faults in the higher nature may be less venial

than those in the lower, and to the eye of Him who is Love, a sin against Love may seem a hundred times more base. No form of vice, not worldliness, not greed of gold, not drunkenness itself, does more to un-Christianise society than evil temper. For embittering life, for breaking up communities, for destroying the most sacred relationships, for devastating homes, for withering up men and women, for taking the bloom off childhood; in short, for sheer gratuitous misery-producing power, this influence stands alone. Look at the Elder Brother, moral, hard-working, patient, dutiful —let him get all credit for his virtues—look at this man, this baby, sulking outside his own father's door. "He was angry," we read, "and would not go in." Look at the effect upon the father, upon the servants, upon the happiness of the guests. Judge of the effect upon the Prodigal—and how many prodigals are kept out of the Kingdom of God by the unlovely characters of those who profess to be inside? Analyse, as a study in Temper, the thundercloud itself as it gathers upon the Elder Brother's brow. What is it made of? Jealousy, anger, pride, uncharity, cruelty, self-righteousness, touchiness, doggedness, sullenness—these are the ingredients of this dark and loveless soul. In varying proportions, also, these are the ingredients of all ill-temper. Judge if such sins of the disposition are not worse to live in, and for others to live with, than sins of the body. Did Christ indeed not answer the question Himself when He said, "I say unto you, that the publicans and the harlots go into the Kingdom of Heaven before you." There is really no place in Heaven for a disposition like this. A man with such a mood could only make Heaven miserable for all the people in it. Except therefore, such a man be born again, he cannot, he simply *cannot*, enter the Kingdom of Heaven. For it is perfectly certain—and you will not misunderstand me—that to enter Heaven a man must take it with him.

You will see then why Temper is significant. It is not in what it is alone, but in what it reveals. This is why I take the liberty now of speaking of it with such unusual plainness. It is a test for love, a symptom, a revelation of an unloving nature at bottom. It is the intermittent fever which bespeaks unintermittent disease within; the occasional bubble escaping to the surface which betrays some rottenness underneath; a sample of the most hidden products of the soul dropped involuntarily when off one's guard; in a word, the lightning form of a hundred hideous and un-Christian sins. For a want of patience, a want of kindness, a want of generosity, a want of courtesy, a want of unselfishness, are all instantaneously symbolised in one flash of Temper.

Hence it is not enough to deal with the Temper. We must go to the source, and change the inmost nature, and the angry humours will die away of themselves. Souls are made sweet not by taking the acid fluids out, but by putting something in—a great Love, a new Spirit, the Spirit of Christ. Christ, the Spirit of Christ, interpenetrating ours, sweetens, purifies, transforms all. This only can eradicate what is wrong, work a chemical change, renovate and regenerate, and rehabilitate the inner man. Will-power does not change men. Time does not change men. Christ does. Therefore "Let that mind be in you which was also in Christ Jesus." Some of us have not much time to lose. Remember, once more, that this is a matter of life or death. I cannot help speaking urgently, for myself, for yourselves. "Whoso shall offend one of these little ones, which believe in me, it were better for him that a millstone were hanged about his neck, and that he were drowned in the depth of the sea." That is to say, it is the deliberate verdict of the Lord Jesus that it is better not to live than not to love. *It is better not to live than not to love.*

Guilelessness and *Sincerity* may be dismissed almost with a word. Guilelessness is the grace for suspicious people. And the possession of it is the great secret of personal influence. You will find, if you think for a moment, that the people who influence you are people who believe in you. In an atmosphere of suspicion men shrivel up; but in that atmosphere they expand and find encouragement and educative fellowship. It is a wonderful thing that here and there in this hard, uncharitable world there should still be left a few rare souls who think no evil. This is the great unworldliness. Love "thinketh no evil," imputes no motive, sees the bright side, puts the best construction on every action. What a delightful state of mind to live in! What a stimulus and bene- diction even to meet with it for a day! To be trusted is to be saved. And if we try to influence or elevate others, we shall soon see that success is in proportion to their belief of our belief in them. For the respect of another is the first restoration of the self-respect a man has lost; our ideal of what he is becomes to him the hope and pattern of what he may become.

"Love rejoiceth not in iniquity, but rejoiceth in the truth." I have called this *Sincerity* from the words rendered in the Authorised Version by "rejoiceth in the truth." And, certainly, were this the real translation, nothing could be more just. For he who loves will love Truth not less than men. He will rejoice in the Truth —rejoice not in what he has been taught to believe; not in this Church's doctrine or in that; not in this ism or in that ism; but "in *the Truth*." He will accept only what is real; he will strive to get at facts; he will search for *Truth* with a humble and unbiased mind, and cherish whatever he finds at any sacrifice. But the more literal translation of the Revised Version calls for just such a sacrifice for truth's sake here. For what Paul really meant is, as we there read, "Rejoiceth not in unrighteousness, but rejoiceth with the truth," a quality which probably no one English word—and certainly not *Sincerity*—adequately defines. It includes, perhaps more strictly, the self-restraint which refuses to make capital out of others' faults; the charity which delights not in exposing the weakness of others, but "covereth all things"; the sincerity of purpose which endeavours to see things as they are, and rejoices to find them better than suspicion feared or calumny denounced.

So much for the analysis of Love. Now the business of our lives is to have these things fitted into our characters. That is the supreme work to which we need to address ourselves in this world, to learn Love. Is life not full of opportunities for learning Love? Every man and woman every day has a thousand of them. The world is not a play-ground; it is a school-room. Life is not a holiday, but an education. And the one eternal lesson for us all is *how better we can love*. What makes a man a good cricketer? Practice. What makes a man a good artist, a good sculptor, a good musician? Practice. What makes a man a good linguist, a good stenographer? Practice. What makes a man a good man? Practice. Nothing else. There is nothing capricious about religion. We do not get the soul in different ways, under different laws, from those in which we get the body and the mind. If a man does not exercise his arm he develops no biceps muscle; and if a man does not exercise his soul, he acquires no muscle in his soul, no strength of character, no vigour of moral fibre, nor beauty of spiritual growth. Love is not a thing of enthusiastic emotion. It is a rich, strong, manly, vigorous expression of the whole round Christian character—the Christ-like nature in its fullest development. And the constituents of this great character are only to be built up by ceaseless practice.

What was Christ doing in the carpenter's shop? Practising. Though perfect, we read that He *learned* obedience. He *increased* in wisdom and in favour with God and man. Do not quarrel therefore with your lot in life. Do not complain of its never-ceasing cares, its petty environment, the vexations you have to stand, the small and sordid souls you have to live and work with. Above all, do not resent temptation; do not be perplexed because it seems to thicken round you more and more, and ceases neither for effort nor for agony nor for prayer. That is the practice which God appoints you; and it is having its work in making you patient, and humble, and generous, and unselfish, and kind, and courteous. Do not grudge the hand that is moulding the still too shapeless image within you. It is growing more beautiful though you see it not, and every touch of temptation may add to its perfection. Therefore keep in the midst of life. Do not isolate yourself. Be among men, and among things, and among troubles, and difficulties, and obstacles. You remember Goethe's words: *Es bildet ein Talent sich in der Stille, Doch ein Character in dem Strom der Welt.* "Talent develops itself in solitude; character in the stream of life." Talent develops itself in solitude—the talent of prayer, of faith, of meditation, of seeing the unseen; Character grows in the stream of the world's life. That chiefly is where men are to learn love.

How? Now, how? To make it easier, I have named a few of the elements of love. But these are only elements. Love itself can never be defined. Light is a something more than the sum of its ingredients—a glowing, dazzling, tremulous ether. And love is something more than all its elements—a palpitating, quivering, sensitive, living thing. By synthesis of all the colours men can make whiteness, they cannot make light. By synthesis of all the virtues, men can make virtue, they cannot make love. How then are we to have this transcendent living whole conveyed into our souls? We brace our wills to secure it. We try to copy those who have it. We lay down rules about it. We watch. We pray. But these things alone will not bring Love into our nature. Love is an *effect*. And only as we fulfil the right condition can we have the effect produced. Shall I tell you what the *cause* is?

If you turn to the Revised Version of the First Epistle of John you will find these words: "We love, because He first loved us." "We love," not "We love *Him*." That is the way the old Version has it, and it is quite wrong. "We *love*—because He first loved us." Look at that word "because." It is the *cause* of which I have spoken. "*Because* He first loved us," the effect follows that we love, we love Him, we love all men. We cannot help it. Because He loved us, we love, we love everybody. Our heart is slowly changed. Contemplate the love of Christ, and you will love. Stand before that mirror, reflect Christ's character, and you will be changed into the same image from tenderness to tenderness. There is no other way. You cannot love to order. You can only look at the lovely object, and fall in love with it, and grow into likeness to it. And so look at this Perfect

Character, this Perfect Life. Look at the great Sacrifice as He laid down Himself, all through life, and upon the Cross of Calvary; and you must love Him. And loving Him, you must become like Him. Love begets Love. It is a process of induction. Put a piece of iron in the presence of a magnetised body, and that piece of iron for a time becomes magnetised. It is charged with an attractive force in the mere presence of the original force, and as long as you leave the two side by side, they are both magnets alike. Remain side by side with Him who loved us. and gave Himself for us, and you too will become a centre of power, a permanently attractive force; and like Him you will draw all men unto you, like Him you will be drawn unto all men. That is the inevitable effect of Love. Any man who fulfils that cause must have that effect produced in him. Try to give up the idea that religion comes to us by chance, or by mystery, or by caprice. It comes to us by natural law, or by supernatural law, for all law is Divine. Edward Irving went to see a dying boy once, and when he entered the room he just put his hand on the sufferer's head, and said, "My boy, God loves you," and went away. And the boy started from his bed, and called out to the people in the house, "God loves me! God loves me!" It changed that boy. The sense that God loved him overpowered him, melted him down, and began the creating of a new heart in him. And that is how the love of God melts down the unlovely heart in man, and begets in him the new creature, who is patient and humble and gentle and unselfish. And there is no other way to get it. There is no mystery about it. We love others, we love everybody, we love our enemies, because He first loved us.

The Defence

Now I have a closing sentence or two to add about Paul's reason for singling out love as the supreme possession. It is a very remarkable reason. In a single word it is this: *it lasts*. "Love," urges Paul, "never faileth." Then he begins again one of his marvellous lists of the great things of the day, and exposes them one by one. He runs over the things that men thought were going to last, and shows that they are all fleeting, temporary, passing away.

"Whether there be prophecies, they shall fail." It was the mother's ambition for her boy in those days that he should become a prophet. For hundreds of years God had never spoken by means of any prophet, and at that time the prophet was greater than the king. Men waited wistfully for another messenger to come, and hung upon his lips when he appeared as upon the very voice of God. Paul says, "Whether there be prophecies they shall fail." This Book is full of prophecies. One by one they have "failed"; that is, having been fulfilled their work is finished; they have nothing more to do now in the world except to feed a devout man's faith.

Then Paul talks about tongues. That was another thing that was greatly coveted. "Whether there be tongues, they shall cease." As we all know, many centuries have passed since tongues have been known in this world. They have ceased. Take it in any sense you like. Take it, for illustration merely, as languages in general—a sense which was not in Paul's mind at all, and which though it cannot give us the specific lesson will point the general truth. Consider the words in which these chapters were written—Greek. It has gone.

Take the Latin—the other great tongue of those days. It ceased long ago. Look at the Indian language. It is ceasing. The language of Wales, of Ireland, of the Scottish Highlands is dying before our eyes. The most popular book in the English tongue at the present time, except the Bible, is one of Dickens's works, his *Pickwick Papers*. It is largely written in the language of London street-life; and experts assure us that in fifty years it will be unintelligible to the average English reader.

Then Paul goes farther, and with even greater boldness adds, "Whether there be knowledge, it shall vanish away." The wisdom of the ancients, where is it? It is wholly gone. A schoolboy to-day knows more than Sir Isaac Newton knew. His knowledge has vanished away. You put yesterday's paper in the fire. Its knowledge has vanished away. You buy the old editions of the great encyclopædias for a few pence. Their knowledge has vanished away. Look how the coach has been superseded by the use of steam. Look how electricity has superseded that, and swept a hundred almost new inventions into oblivion. One of the greatest living authorities, Sir William Thomson, said the other day, "The steam-engine is passing away." "Whether there be knowledge, it shall vanish away." At every workshop you will see, in the back yard, a heap of old iron, a few wheels, a few levers, a few cranks, broken and eaten with rust. Twenty years ago that was the pride of the city. Men flocked in from the country to see the great invention ; now it is superseded, its day is done. And all the boasted science and philosophy of this day will soon be old. But yesterday, in the University of Edinburgh, the greatest figure in the faculty was Sir James Simpson, the discoverer of chloroform. The other day his successor and nephew, Professor Simpson, was asked by the librarian of the University to go to the library and pick out books on his subject that were no longer needed. And his reply to the librarian was this: " Take every text book that is more than ten years old, and put it down in the cellar." Sir James Simpson was a great authority only a few years ago: men came from all parts of the earth to consult him; and almost the whole teaching of that time is consigned by the science of to-day to oblivion. And in every branch of science it is the same. "Now we know in part. We see through a glass darkly."

Can you tell me anything that is going to last? Many things Paul did not condescend to name. He did not mention money, fortune, fame; but he picked out the great things of his time, the things the best men thought had something in them, and brushed them peremptorily aside. Paul had no charge against these things in themselves. All he said about them was that they would not last. They were great things, but not supreme things. They were things beyond them. What we are stretches past what we do, beyond what we possess. Many things that men denounce as sins are not sins; but they are temporary. And that is a favourite argument of the New Testament. John says of the world, not that it is wrong, but simply that it "passeth away." There is a great deal in the world that is delightful and beautiful; there is a great deal in it that is great and engrossing; but it will not last. All that is in the world, the lust of the eye, the lust of the flesh, and the pride of life, are but for a little while. Love not the world therefore. Nothing that it contains is worth the life and consecration of an immortal soul. The immortal soul must give itself to something that is immortal. And the only immortal things are these: "Now abideth faith, hope, love, but the greatest of these is love."

Some think the time will come when two of these three things will also pass away—faith into sight, hope into fruition. Paul does not say so. We know but little now about the conditions of the life that is to come. But what is certain is that Love must last. God, the Eternal God, is Love. Covet therefore that everlasting gift, that one thing which it is certain is going to stand, that one coinage which will be current in the Universe when all the other coinages of all the nations of the world shall be useless and unhonoured. You will give yourselves to many things, give yourselves first to Love. Hold things in their proportion. *Hold things in their proportion.* Let at least the first great object of our lives be to achieve the character defended in these words, the character,—and it is the character of Christ— which is built round Love.

I have said this thing is eternal. Did you ever notice how continually John associates love and faith with eternal life? I was not told when I was a boy that "God so loved the world that He gave His only begotten Son, that whosoever

believeth in Him should have everlasting life."
What I was told, I remember, was, that God
so loved the world that, if I trusted in Him,
I was to have a thing called peace, or I was to
have rest, or I was to have joy, or I was to have
safety. But I had to find out for myself that
whosoever trusteth in Him—that is, whosoever
loveth Him, for trust is only the avenue to
Love—hath everlasting *life*. The Gospel offers
a man life. Never offer men a thimbleful of
Gospel. Do not offer them merely joy, or
merely peace, or merely rest, or merely safety;
tell them how Christ came to give men a more
abundant life than they have, a life abundant
in love, and therefore abundant in salvation
for themselves, and large in enterprise for the
alleviation and redemption of the world. Then
only can the Gospel take hold of the whole of
a man, body, soul, and spirit, and give to each
part of his nature its exercise and reward.
Many of the current Gospels are addressed only
to a part of man's nature. They offer peace,
not life; faith, not Love; justification, not
regeneration. And men slip back again from
such religion because it has never really held
them. Their nature was not all in it. It offered
no deeper and gladder life-current than the life

that was lived before. Surely it stands to reason that only a fuller love can compete with the love of the world.

To love abundantly is to live abundantly, and to love for ever is to live for ever. Hence, eternal life is inextricably bound up with love. We want to live for ever for the same reason that we want to live to-morrow. Why do you want to live to-morrow? It is because there is some one who loves you, and whom you want to see to-morrow, and be with, and love back. There is no other reason why we should live on than that we love and are beloved. It is when a man has no one to love him that he commits suicide. So long as he has friends, those who love him and whom he loves, he will live; because to live is to love. Be it but the love of a dog, it will keep him in life; but let that go and he has no contact with life, no reason to live. The "energy of life" has failed. Eternal life also is to know God, and God is love. This is Christ's own definition. Ponder it. "This is life eternal, that they might know Thee the only true God, and Jesus Christ whom Thou hast sent." Love must be eternal. It is what God is. On the last analysis, then, love is Life. Love never faileth, and life never faileth, so long as there is love. That is the philosophy of what Paul is showing us; the reason why in the nature of things Love should be the supreme thing—because it is going to last; because in the nature of things it is an Eternal Life. That Life is a thing that we are living now, not that we get when we die; that we shall have a poor chance of getting when we die unless we are living now. No worse fate can befall a man in this world than to live and grow old alone, unloving and unloved. To be lost is to live in an unregenerate condition, loveless and unloved; and to be saved is to love; and he that dwelleth in love dwelleth already in God. For God is love.

Now I have all but finished. How many of you will join me in reading this chapter once a week for the next three months? A man did that once and it changed his whole life. Will you do it? It is for the greatest thing in the world. You might begin by reading it every day, especially the verses which describe the perfect character. "Love suffereth long, and is kind; love envieth not; love vaunteth not itself." Get these ingredients into your life. Then everything that you do is eternal. It is worth doing. It is worth giving time to. No

man can become a saint in his sleep; and to
fulfil the conditions required demands a
certain amount of prayer and meditation and
time, just as improvement in any direction,
bodily or mental, requires preparation and care.
Address yourself to that one thing; at any
cost have this transcendent character exchanged
for yours. You will find as you look back
upon your life that the moments that stand
out, the moments when you have really lived,
are the moments when you have done things in
a spirit of love. As memory scans the past,
above and beyond all transitory pleasures of
life, there leap forward those supreme hours
when you have been enabled to do unnoticed
kindnesses to those around about you, things
too trifling to speak about, but which you feel
have entered into your eternal life. I have seen
almost all the beautiful things that God has
made; I have enjoyed almost every pleasure
that He has planned for man; and yet as I look
back I see standing out above all the life that
has gone four or five short experiences when
the love of God reflected itself in some poor
imitation, some small act of love of mine, and
these seem to be things which alone of all one's
life abide. Everything else in all our lives is

transitory. Every other good is visionary. But the acts of love which no man knows about, or can ever know about—they never fail.

In the Book of Matthew, where the Judgment Day is depicted for us in the imagery of One seated upon a throne, and dividing the sheep from the goats, the test of a man is then not, "How have I believed?" but "How have I loved?" The test of religion, the final test of religion, is not religiousness, but Love. I say the final test of religion at that great Day is not religiousness, but Love; not what I have done, not what I have believed, not what I have achieved, but how I have discharged the common charities of life. Sins of commission in that awful indictment are not even referred to. By what we have not done, *by sins of ommision*, we are judged. It could not be otherwise. For the withholding of love is the negation of the spirit of Christ, the proof that we never knew Him, that for us He lived in vain. It means that He suggested nothing in all our thoughts, that He inspired nothing in all our lives, that we were once near enough to Him to be seized with the spell of His compassion for the world. It means that:

" I lived for myself, I thought for myself,
     For myself, and none beside—
Just as if Jesus had never lived,
     As if He had never died."

It is the Son of *Man* before whom the nations
of the world shall be gathered. It is in the
presence of *Humanity* that we shall be charged.
And the spectacle itself, the mere sight of it,
will silently judge each one. Those will be
there whom we have met and helped; or there,
the unpitied multitude whom we neglected or
despised. No other Witness need be summoned.
No other charge than lovelessness shall be
preferred. Be not deceived. The words which
all of us shall one Day hear, sound not of
theology but of life, not of churches and saints
but of the hungry and the poor, not of creeds
and doctrines but of shelter and clothing, not
of Bibles and prayer-books but of cups of cold
water in the name of Christ. Thank God the
Christianity of to-day is coming nearer the
world's need. Live to help that on. Thank God
men know better, by a hairsbreadth, what
religion is, what God is, who Christ is, where
Christ is. Who is Christ? He who fed the
hungry, clothed the naked, visited the sick.

And where is Christ? Where?—whoso shall
receive a little child in My name receiveth Me.
And who are Christ's? Every one that loveth
is born of God.

THE
PROGRAMME OF CHRISTIANITY

To Preach Good Tidings unto the Meek:
To Bind up the Broken-Hearted:
To Proclaim Liberty to the Captives and the Opening
of the Prison to Them that are Bound:
To Proclaim the Acceptable Year of the Lord, and
the Day of Vengeance of our God:
To Comfort all that Mourn:
To Appoint unto them that Mourn in Zion:
To Give unto them—
Beauty for Ashes,
The Oil of Joy for Mourning,
The Garment of Praise for the Spirit of Heaviness.

THE
PROGRAMME OF CHRISTIANITY

"WHAT does God do all day?" once asked
a little boy. One could wish that more
grown-up people would ask so very real a
question. Unfortunately, most of us are not
even boys in religious intelligence, but only
very unthinking children. It no more occurs
to us that God is engaged in any particular
work in the world than it occurs to a little child
that its father does anything except be its
father. Its father may be a Cabinet Minister
absorbed in the nation's work, or an inventor
deep in schemes for the world's good; but to
this master-egoist he is father, and nothing
more. Childhood, whether in the physical or
moral world, is the great self-centred period
of life; and a personal God who satisfies
personal ends is all that for a long time many
a Christian understands.

But as clearly as there comes to the growing
child a knowledge of its father's part in the
world, and a sense of what real life means, there

must come to every Christian whose growth is true some richer sense of the meaning of Christianity and a larger view of Christ's purpose for mankind. To miss this is to miss the whole splendour and glory of Christ's religion. Next to losing the sense of a personal Christ, the worst evil that can befall a Christian is to have no sense of anything else. To grow up in complacent belief that God has no business in this great groaning world of human beings except to attend to a few saved souls is the negation of all religion. The first great epoch in a Christian's life, after the awe and wonder of its dawn, is when there breaks into his mind some sense that Christ has a purpose for mankind, a purpose beyond him and his needs, beyond the churches and their creeds, beyond Heaven and its saints—a purpose which embraces every man and woman born, every kindred and nation formed, which regards not their spiritual good alone but their welfare in every part, their progress, their health, their work, their wages, their happiness in this present world.

What, then, does Christ do all day? By what further conception shall we augment the selfish view of why Christ lived and died?

I shall mislead no one, I hope, if I say—for I wish to put the social side of Christianity in its strongest light—that Christ did not come into the world to give men religion. He never mentioned the word religion. Religion was in the world before Christ came, and it lives to-day in a million souls who have never heard His name. *What God does all day* is not to sit waiting in churches for people to come and worship Him. It is true that God is in churches and in all kinds of churches, and is found by many in churches more immediately than anywhere else. It is also true that while Christ did not give men religion He gave a new direction to the religious aspiration bursting forth then and now and always from the whole world's heart. But it was His purpose to enlist these aspirations on behalf of some definite practical good. The religious people of those days did nothing with their religion except attend to its observances. Even the priest, after he had been to the temple, thought his work was done; when he met the wounded man he passed by on the other side. Christ reversed all this—tried to reverse it, for He is only now beginning to succeed. The tendency of the religions of all time has been to care more for religion than for humanity; Christ cared more for humanity than for religion—rather His care for humanity was the chief expression of His religion. He was not indifferent to observances, but the practices of the people bulked in His thoughts before the practices of the Church. It has been pointed out as a blemish on the immortal allegory of Bunyan that the Pilgrim never *did* anything, anything but save his soul. The remark is scarcely fair, for the allegory is designedly the story of a soul in a single relation; and besides, he did do a little. But the warning may well be weighed. The Pilgrim's one thought, his work by day, his dream by night, was *escape*. He took little part in the world through which he passed. He was a *Pilgrim* travelling through it; his business was to get through safe. Whatever this is, it is not Christianity. Christ's conception of Christianity was heavens removed from that of a man setting out from the City of Destruction to save his soul. It was rather that of a man dwelling amidst the Destructions of the City and planning escapes for the souls of others —escapes not to the other world, but to purity and peace and righteousness in this. In reality Christ never said, "Save your soul." It is a mistranslation which says that. What He said was, "Save your life." And this not because the first is nothing, but only because it is so very great a thing that only the second can accomplish it. But the new word altruism—the translation of "love thy neighbour as thyself"—is slowly finding its way into current Christian speech. The People's Progress, not less than the Pilgrim's Progress, is daily becoming a graver concern to the Church. A popular theology with unselfishness as part at least of its root, a theology which appeals no longer to fear, but to the generous heart in man, has already dawned, and more clearly than ever men are beginning to see what Christ really came into this world to do.

What Christ came here for was to make a better world. The world in which we live is an unfinished world. It is not wise, it is not happy, it is not pure, it is not good—it is not even sanitary. Humanity is little more than raw material. Almost everything has yet to be done to it. Before the days of Geology people thought the earth was finished. It is by no means finished. The work of Creation is going on. Before the spectroscope, men thought the universe was finished. We know now it is just beginning. And this teeming universe of men in which we live has almost all its finer colour and beauty yet to take. Christ came to complete it. The fires of its passion were not yet cool; their heat had to be transformed into finer energies. The ideals for its future were all to shape, the forces to realise them were not yet born. The poison of its sins had met no antidote, the gloom of its doubt no light, the weight of its sorrow no rest. These the Saviour of the world, the Light of men, would do and be. This, roughly, was His scheme.

Now this was a prodigious task—to recreate the world. How was it to be done? God's way of making worlds is to make them make themselves. When he made the earth He made a rough ball of matter and supplied it with a multitude of tools to mould it into form—the rain-drop to carve it, the glacier to smooth it, the river to nourish it, the flower to adorn it. God works always with agents, and this is our way when we want any great thing done, and this was Christ's way when He undertook the finishing of Humanity. He had a vast intractable mass of matter to deal with, and He required a multitude of tools. Christ's tools were men. Hence His first business in the world was to make a collection of men. In other words, He founded a Society.

The Founding of the Society

It is a somewhat startling thought—it will not be misunderstood—that Christ probably did not save many people while He was here. Many an evangelist in that direction has done much more. He never intended to finish the world single-handed, but announced from the first that others would not only take part, but do " greater things " than He. For amazing as was the attention He was able to give to individuals, this was not the whole aim He had in view. His immediate work was to enlist men in His enterprise, to rally them into a great company or Society for the carrying out of His plans.

The name by which this Society was known was *The Kingdom of God*. Christ did not coin this name; it was an old expression, and good men had always hoped and prayed that some such Society would be born in their midst. But it was never either defined or set agoing in earnest until Christ made its realisation the passion of His life.

How keenly He felt regarding His task, how enthusiastically He set about it, every page of His life bears witness. All reformers have one or two great words which they use incessantly, and by mere reiteration imbed indelibly in the thought and history of their time. Christ's great word was the Kingdom of God. Of all the words of His that have come down to us this is by far the commonest. One hundred times it occurs in the Gospels. When He preached He had almost always this for a text. His sermons were explanations of the aims of His Society, of the different things it was like, of whom its membership consisted, what they were to do or to be, or not do or not be. And even when He does not actually use the word, it is easy to see that all He said and did had reference to this. Philosophers talk about thinking in categories—the mind living, as it were, in a particular room with its own special furniture, pictures, and view-points, these giving a consistent direction and colour to all that is there thought or expressed. It was in the category of the Kingdom that Christ's thought moved. Though one time, He said

He came to save the lost, or at another time to give men life, or to do His Father's will, these were all included among the objects of His Society.

No one can ever know what Christianity is till he has grasped this leading thought in the mind of Christ. Peter and Paul have many wonderful and necessary things to tell us about what Christ was and did; but we are looking now at what Christ's own thought was. Do not think this is a mere modern theory. These are His own life-plans taken from His own lips. Do not allow any isolated text, even though it seems to sum up for you the Christian life, to keep you from trying to understand Christ's Programme as a whole. The perspective of Christ's teaching is not everything, but without it everything will be distorted and untrue. There is much good in a verse, but often much evil. To see some small soul pirouetting thoughout life on a single text, and judging all the world because it cannot find a partner, is not a Christian sight. Christianity does not grudge such souls their comfort. What it grudges is that they make Christ's Kingdom uninhabitable to thoughtful minds. Be sure that whenever the religion of Christ appears small, or forbidding, or narrow, or inhuman, you are dealing not with the whole—which is a matchless moral symmetry—nor even with an arch or column—for every detail is perfect —but with some cold stone removed from its place and suggesting nothing of the glorious structure from which it came.

Tens of thousands of persons who are familiar with religious truths have not noticed yet that Christ ever founded a Society at all. The reason is partly that people have read texts instead of reading their Bible, partly that they have studied Theology instead of studying Christianity, and partly because of the noiselessness and invisibility of the Kingdom of God itself. Nothing truer was ever said of this Kingdom than that "It cometh without observation." Its first discovery, therefore, comes to the Christian with all the force of a revelation. The sense of belonging to such a Society transforms life. It is the difference between being a solitary knight tilting single-handed, and often defeated, at whatever enemy one chances to meet on one's little acre of life, and the *feel* of belonging to a mighty army marching throughout all time to a certain victory. This note of universality given to even the humblest work we do, this sense of comradeship, this link with history, this thought of a definite campaign, this promise of success, is the possession of every obscurest unit in the Kingdom of God.

The Programme of the Society

Hundreds of years before Christ's Society was formed, its Programme had been issued to the world. I cannot think of any scene in history more dramatic than when Jesus entered the church in Nazareth and read it to the people. Not that when He appropriated to Himself that venerable fragment from Isaiah He was uttering a manifesto or announcing His formal Programme. Christ never did things formally. We think of the words, as He probably thought of them, not in their old-world historical significance, nor as a full expression of His future aims, but as a summary of great moral facts now and always to be realised in the world since he appeared.

Remember as you read the words to what grim reality they refer. Recall what Christ's

problem really was, what His Society was
founded for. This Programme deals with a
real world. Think of it as you read—not of
the surface-world, but of the world as it is, as it
sins and weeps, and curses and suffers and
sends up its long cry to God. Limit it if you
like to the world around your door, but think
of it—of the city and the hospital and the
dungeon and the graveyard, of the sweating-
shop and the pawn-shop and the drink-shop;
think of the cold, the cruelty, the fever, the
famine, the ugliness, the loneliness, the pain.
And then try to keep down the lump in your
throat as you take up His Programme and
read—

To Bind up the Broken-Hearted:
To Proclaim Liberty to the Captives:
To Comfort all that Mourn:
To Give unto them—
          Beauty for Ashes,
          The Oil of Joy for Mourning,
          The Garment of Praise for the Spirit of
            Heaviness.

What an exchange—Beauty for Ashes, Joy
for Mourning, Liberty for Chains! No marvel

"the eyes of all them that were in the synagogue were fastened on Him" as He read; or that they "wondered at the gracious words which proceeded out of His lips." Only one man in that congregation, only one man in the world to-day could hear these accents with dismay—the man, the culprit, who has said hard words of Christ.

We are all familiar with the protest, "Of course"—as if there were no other alternative to a person of culture—"Of course I am not a Christian, but I always speak *respectfully* of Christianity." Respectfully of Christianity! No remark fills one's soul with such sadness. One can understand a man as he reads these words being stricken speechless; one can see the soul within him rise to a white heat as each fresh benediction falls upon his ear and drives him, a half-mad enthusiast, to bear them to the world. But in what school has he learned of Christ who offers the Saviour of the world his respect?

Men repudiate Christ's religion because they think it a small and limited thing, a scheme with no large human interests to commend it to this great social age. I ask you to note that there is not one burning interest of the human race which is not represented here. What are the great words of Christianity according to this Programme! Take as specimens these:

> *Liberty,*
> *Comfort,*
> *Beauty,*
> *Joy.*

These are among the greatest words of life. Give them their due extension, the significance which Christ undoubtedly saw in them and which Christianity undoubtedly yields, and there is almost no great want or interest of mankind which they do not cover.

These are not only the greatest words of life, but they are the best. This Programme, to those who have misread Christianity, is a series of surprises. Observe the most prominent note in it. It is *gladness*. Its first word is "good-tidings," its last is "joy." The saddest words of life are also there—but there as the diseases which Christianity comes to cure. No life that is occupied with such an enterprise could be other than radiant. The contribution of Christianity to the joy of living, perhaps even more to the joy of *thinking*, is unspeakable. The joyful life is the life of the larger mission,

the disinterested life, the life of the overflow
from self, the "more abundant life" which
comes from following Christ. And the joy
of thinking is the larger thinking, the thinking
of the man who holds in his hand some Programme for Humanity. The Christian is the
only man who has any Programme at all—any
Programme either for the world or for himself. Goethe, Byron, Carlyle taught Humanity
much, but they had no Programme for it.
Byron's thinking was suffering; Carlyle's,
despair. Christianity alone exults. The belief
in the universe as moral, the interpretation of
history as progress, the faith in good as eternal,
in evil as self-consuming, in humanity as
evolving—these Christian ideas have transformed the malady of thought into a bounding
hope. It was no sentiment but a conviction
matured amid calamity and submitted to the
tests of life that inspired the great modern
poet of optimism to proclaim:

"Gladness be with thee, Helper of the world!
 I think this is the authentic sign and seal
 Of Godship, that ever waxes glad,
 And more glad, until gladness blossoms,
  bursts

Into a rage to suffer for mankind
And recommence at sorrow."

But that is not all. Man's greatest needs are
often very homely. And it is almost as much
in its fearless recognition of the commonplace
woes of life, and its deliberate offerings to
minor needs, that the claims of Christianity
to be a religion for Humanity stand. Look,
for instance, at the closing sentence of this
Programme. Who would have expected to
find among the special objects of Christ's
solicitude the *Spirit of Heaviness*? Supreme
needs, many and varied, had been already dealt
with on this Programme; many applicants had
been met; the list is about to close. Suddenly
the writer remembers the nameless malady of
the poor—that mysterious disease which the
rich share but cannot alleviate, which is too
subtle for doctors, too incurable for Parlia-
ments, too unpicturesque for philanthropy, too
common even for sympathy. Can Christ meet
that?

If Christianity could even deal with the
world's Depression, could cure mere dull
spirits, it would be the Physician of Humanity.
But it can. It has the secret, a hundred secrets,

for the lifting of the world's gloom. It cannot immediately remove the physiological causes of dullness—though obedience to its principles can do an infinity to prevent them, and its inspirations can do even more to lift the mind above them. But where the causes are moral or mental or social, the remedy is in every Christian's hand. Think of any one at this moment whom the Spirit of Heaviness haunts. You think of a certain old woman. But you know for a fact that you can cure her. You did so, perfectly, only a week ago. A mere visit, and a little present, or the visit without any present, set her up for seven long days, and seven long nights. The machinery of the Kingdom is very simple and very silent, and the most silent parts do most, and we all believe so little in the medicines of Christ that we do not know what ripples of healing are set in motion when we simply smile on one another. Christianity wants nothing so much in the world as sunny people, and the old are hungrier for love than for bread, and the Oil of Joy is very cheap, and if you can help the poor on with a Garment of Praise, it will be better for them than blankets.

Or perhaps you know someone else who is

dull—not an old woman this time but a very rich and important man. But you also know perfectly what makes him dull. It is either his riches or his importance. Christianity can cure either of these—though you may not be the person to apply the cure—at a single hearing. Or here is a third case, one of your own servants. It is a case of *monotony*. Prescribe more variety, leisure, recreation—anything to relieve the wearing strain. A fourth case—your most honoured guest: Condition—leisure, health, accomplishments, means; Disease—Spiritual Obesity; Treatment—talent to be put out to usury. And so on down the whole range of life's dejection and *ennui*.

Perhaps you tell me this is not Christianity at all; that everybody could do that. The curious thing is that everybody does not. Good-will to men came into the world with Christ, and wherever that is found, in Christian or heathen land, there Christ is, and there His spirit works. And if you say that the chief end of Christianity is not the world's happiness, I agree; it was never meant to be; but the strange fact is that, without making it its chief end, it wholly and infallibly, and quite universally, leads to it. Hence the note of Joy, though not the highest on Christ's Programme, is a loud and ringing note, and none who serve in His Society can be long without its music. Time was when a Christian used to apologise for being happy. But the day has always been when he ought to apologise for being miserable.

Christianity, you will observe, really works. And it succeeds not only because it is divine, but because it is so very human—because it is commonsense. Why should the Garment of Praise destroy the Spirit of Heaviness? Because an old woman cannot sing and cry at the same moment. The Society of Christ is a sane Society. Its methods are rational. The principle in the old woman's case is simply that one emotion destroys another. Christianity works, as a railway man would say, with points. It switches souls from valley lines to mountain lines, not stemming the currents of life but diverting them. In the rich man's case the principle of cure is different, but it is again principle, not necromancy. His spirit of heaviness is caused, like any other heaviness, by the earth's attraction. Take away the earth and you take away the attraction. But if Christianity can do anything it can take away the earth. By the wider extension of the horizon which it gives, by the new standard of values, by the mere setting of life's small pomps and interests and admirations in the light of the Eternal, it dissipates the world with a breath. All that tends to abolish worldliness tends to abolish unrest, and hence, in the rush of modern life, one far-reaching good of all even commonplace Christian preaching, all Christian literature, all which holds the world doggedly to the idea of a God and a future life, and reminds mankind of Infinity and Eternity.

Side by side with these influences, yet taking the world at a wholly different angle, works another great Christian force. How many opponents of religion are aware that one of the specific objects of Christ's Society is Beauty? The charge of vulgarity against Christianity is an old one. If it means that Christianity deals with the ruder elements in human nature, it is true, and that is its glory. But if it means that it has no respect for the finer qualities, the charge is baseless. For Christianity not only encourages whatsoever things are lovely, but wars against that whole theory of life which would exclude them. It prescribes æstheticism. It proscribes asceticism. And for those who preach to Christians that in these enlightened days they must raise the masses by giving them noble sculptures and beautiful paintings and music and public parks, the answer is that these things are all already being given, and given daily, and with an increasing sense of their importance, by the Society of Christ. Take away from the world the beautiful things which have not come from Christ and you will make it poorer scarcely at all. Take away from modern cities the paintings, the monuments, the music for the people, the museums and the parks which are not the gifts of Christian men and Christian municipalities, and in ninety cases out of a hundred you will leave them unbereft of so much as a well-shaped lamp-post.

It is impossible to doubt that the Decorator of the World shall not continue to serve to His later children, and in ever finer forms, the inspirations of beautiful things. More fearlessly than he has ever done, the Christian of modern life will use the noble spiritual leverages of Art. That this world, the people's world, is a bleak and ugly world, we do not forget; it is ever with us. But we esteem too little the mission of beautiful things in haunting the mind with higher thoughts and begetting the mood which leads to God. Physical beauty makes moral beauty. Loveliness does more than destroy ugliness; it destroys matter. A mere touch of it in a room, in a street, even on a door knocker, is a spiritual force. Ask the working-man's wife, and she will tell you there is a moral effect even in a clean table-cloth. If a barrel-organ in a slum can but drown a curse, let no Christian silence it. The mere light and colour of the wall-advertisements are a gift of God to the poor man's sombre world.

One Christmas-time a poor drunkard told me that he had gone out the night before to take his usual chance of the temptations of the street. Close to his door, at a shop window, an angel—so he said—arrested him. It was a large Christmas-card, a glorious white thing with tinsel wings, and as it glittered in the gas-light it flashed into his soul a sudden thought of Heaven. It recalled the earlier heaven of his infancy, and he thought of his mother in the distant glen, and how it would please her if she got this Christmas angel from her prodigal. With money already pledged to the devil he bought the angel, and with it a new soul and future for himself. That was a real angel. For that day as I saw its tinsel pinions shine in his squalid room I knew what Christ's angels were. They are all beautiful things, which daily in common homes are bearing up heavy souls to God.

But do not misunderstand me. This angel was made of pasteboard: a pasteboard angel can never save a soul. Tinsel reflects the sun, but warms nothing. Our Programme must go deeper. Beauty may arrest the drunkard, but it cannot cure him.

It is here that Christianity asserts itself with a supreme individuality. It is here that it parts company with Civilisation, with Politics, with all secular schemes of Social Reform. In its diagnosis of human nature it finds that which most other systems ignore; which, if they see, they cannot cure; which, left undestroyed, makes every reform futile, and every inspiration vain. That thing is *Sin*. Christanity destroyed, makes every reform futile, and every inspiration vain. That thing is *Sin*. Christianity, of all other philanthropies, recognises that man's devouring need is *Liberty*—liberty to stop sinning; to leave the prison of his passions, and shake off the fetters of his past. To surround *Captives* with statues and pictures, to offer *Them-that-are-Bound* a higher wage or a cleaner street or a few more cubic feet of air per head, is solemn trifling. It is a cleaner soul they want; a purer air, or any air at all, for their higher selves.

And where the cleaner soul is to come from apart from Christ I cannot tell. "By no political alchemy," Herbert Spencer tells us, "can you get golden conduct out of leaden instincts." The power to set the heart right, to renew the springs of action, comes from Christ. The sense of infinite worth of the single soul, and the recoverableness of man at his worst, are the gifts of Christ. The freedom from guilt, the forgiveness of sins, come from Christ's Cross; the hope of immortality springs from Christ's grave. We believe in the gospel of better laws and an improved environment; we hold the religion of Christ to be a social religion; we magnify and call Christian the work of reformers, statesmen, philanthropists, educators, inventors, sanitary officers, and all who directly or remotely aid, abet, or further the higher progress of mankind; but in Him alone, in the fullness of that word, do we see the Saviour of the world.

There are earnest and gifted lives to-day at

work among the poor whose lips at least will not name the name of Christ. I speak of them with respect; their shoe-latchets many of us are not worthy to unloose. But because the creed of the neighbouring mission-hall is a travesty of religion they refuse to acknowledge the power of the living Christ to stop man's sin, of the dying Christ to forgive it. O, narrowness of breadth! Because there are ignorant doctors do I yet rail at medicine or start an hospital of my own? Because the poor raw evangelist, or the narrow ecclesiastic, offer their little all to the poor, shall I repudiate all they do not know of Christ because of the little that they do know? Of gospels for the poor which have not some theory, state it how you will, of personal conversion one cannot have much hope. Personal conversion means for life a personal religion, a personal trust in God, a personal debt to Christ, a personal dedication to His cause. These, brought about how you will, are supreme things to aim at, supreme losses if they are missed. Sanctification will come to masses only as it comes to individual men; and to work with Christ's Programme and ignore Christ is to utilise the sun's light without its energy.

But this is not the only point at which the uniqueness of this Society appears. There is yet another depth of humanity which no other system even attempts to sound. We live in a world not only of sin but of sorrow—

"There is no flock, however watched and
    tended,
    But one dead lamb is there;
There is no home, howe'er defended,
    But has one vacant chair."

When the flock thins, and the chair empties, who is to be near to heal? At that moment the gospels of the world are on trial. In the presence of death how will they act? Act! They are blotted out of existence. Philosophy, Politics, Reforms, are no more. The Picture Galleries close. The Sculptures hide. The Committees disperse. There is crape on the door; the world withdraws. Observe, *it withdraws*. It has no mission.

So awful in its loneliness was this hour that the Romans paid a professional class to step in with its mummeries and try to fill it. But that is Christ's own hour. Next to Righteousness the greatest word of Christianity is Comfort.

Christianity has almost a monopoly of Comfort. Renan was never nearer the mark than when he spoke of the Bible as "the great book of the Consolation of Humanity." Christ's Programme is full of Comfort, studded with Comfort: "to bind up the Broken-Hearted, to Comfort all that mourn, to Give unto them that mourn in Zion." Even the "good tidings" to the "meek" are, in the Hebrew, a message to the "afflicted" or "the poor." The word Gospel itself comes down through the Greek from this very passage, so that whatever else Christ's Gospel means it is first an Evangel for suffering men.

One note in this Programme jars with all the rest. When Christ read from Isaiah that day He never finished the passage. A terrible word, Vengeance, yawned like a precipice across His path; and in the middle of a sentence "He closed the Book, and gave it again to the minister, and sat down." A Day of Vengeance from our God—these were the words before which Christ paused. When the prophet proclaimed it some great historical fulfilment was in his mind. Had the people to whom Christ read been able to understand its ethical equivalents He would probably have read on.

For, so understood, instead of filling the mind
with fear, the thought of this Dread Day
inspires it with a solemn gratitude. The work
of the Avenger is a necessity. It is part of God's
philanthropy.

For I have but touched the surface in speaking
of the sorrow of the world as if it came from
people dying. It comes from people living.
Before ever the Broken-Hearted can be healed a
hundred greater causes of suffering than death
must be destroyed. Before the Captive can be
free a vaster prison than his own sins must be
demolished. There are hells on earth into which
no breath of heaven can ever come; these must
be swept away. There are social soils in which
only unrighteousness can flourish; these must
be broken up.

And that is the work of the Day of Vengeance.
When is that day? It is now. Who is the
Avenger? Law. What Law? Criminal Law,
Sanitary Law, Social Law, Natural Law.
Wherever the poor are trodden upon or tread
upon one another; wherever the air is poison
and the water foul; wherever want stares, and
vice reigns, and rags rot—there the Avenger
takes his stand. Whatever makes it more
difficult for the drunkard to reform, for the

children to be pure, for the widow to earn a
wage, for any of the wheels of progress to
revolve—with these he deals. Delay him not.
He is the messenger of Christ. Despair of him
not, distrust him not. His Day dawns slowly,
but His work is sure. Though evil stalks the
world, it is on the way to execution; though
wrong reigns, it must end in self-combustion.
The very nature of things is God's Avenger;
the very story of civilisation is the history of
Christ's Throne.

Anything that prepares the way for a better
social state is the fit work of the followers of
Christ. Those who work on the more spiritual
levels leave too much unhonoured the slow toil
of multitudes of unchurched souls who prepare
the material or moral environments without
which these higher labours are in vain. Pre-
vention is Christian as well as cure; and
Christianity travels sometimes by the most
circuitous paths. It is given to some to work
for immediate results, and from year to year
they are privileged to reckon up a balance of
success. But these are not always the greatest
in the Kingdom of God. The men who get
no stimulus from any visible reward, whose
lives pass while the objects for which they toil

are still too far away to comfort them; the
men who hold aloof from dazzling schemes
and earn the misunderstanding of the crowd
because they foresee remoter issues, who even
oppose a seeming good because a deeper evil
lurks beyond—these are the *statesmen* of the
Kingdom of God.

The Machinery of the Society

Such in dimmest outline is the Programme of
Christ's Society. Did you know that all this
was going on in the world? Did you know that
Christianity was such a living and purpose-like
thing? Look back to the day when that Programme was given, and you will see that it
was not merely written on paper. Watch the
drama of the moral order rise up, scene after
scene, in history. Study the social evolution
of humanity, the spread of righteousness, the
amelioration of life, the freeing of slaves, the
elevation of woman, the purification of
religion, and ask what these can be if not the
coming of the Kingdom of God on earth. For
it is precisely through the movements of nations

and the lives of men that this Kingdom comes. Christ might have done all this work Himself, with His own hands. But He did not. The crowning wonder of His scheme is that he entrusted it to *men*. It is the supreme glory of humanity that the machinery for its redemption should have been placed within itself. I think the saddest thing in Christ's life was that after founding a Society with aims so glorious He had to go away and leave it.

But in reality He did not leave it. The old theory that God made the world, made it as an inventor would make a machine, and then stood looking on to see it work, has passed away. God is no longer a remote spectator of the natural world, but immanent in it, pervading matter by His present Spirit, and ordering it by His Will. So Christ is immanent in men. His work is to move the hearts and inspire the lives of men, and through such hearts to move and reach the world. Men, only men, can carry out this work. This humanness, this inwardness, of the Kingdom is one reason why some scarcely see that it exists at all. We measure great movement by the loudness of their advertisement, or the place their externals fill in the public eye. This Kingdom has no

externals. The usual methods of propagating
a great cause were entirely discarded by Christ.
The sword He declined; money He had none;
literature He never used; the Church disowned
Him; the State crucified Him. Planting His
ideals in the hearts of a few poor men, He
started them out unheralded to revolutionise
the world. They did it by making friends—and
by making enemies; they went about, did good,
sowed seed, died, and lived again in the lives
of those they helped. These in turn, a fraction
of them, did the same. They met, they prayed,
they talked of Christ, they loved, they went
among other men, and by act and word passed
on their secret. The machinery of the Kingdom
of God is purely social. It acts, not by commandment, but by contagion; not by fiat, but
by friendship. "The Kingdom of God is like
unto leaven, which a woman took and hid in
three measures of meal till the whole was
leavened."

After all, like all great discoveries once they
are made, this seems absolutely the most
feasible method that could have been devised.
Men *must* live among men. Men *must* influence
men. Organisations, institutions, churches,
have too much rigidity for a thing that is to

flood the world. The only fluid in the world is man. War might have won for Christ's cause a passing victory; wealth might have purchased a superficial triumph; political power might have gained a temporary success. But in these there is no note of universality, of solidarity, of immortality. To live through the centuries and pervade the uttermost ends of the earth, to stand while kingdoms tottered and civilisations changed, to survive fallen churches and crumbling creeds—there was no soil for the Kingdom of God like the hearts of common men. Some who have written about this Kingdom have emphasised its moral grandeur, others its universality, others its adaptation to man's needs. One great writer speaks of its prodigious originality, another chiefly notices its success. I confess what almost strikes me most is the miracle of its simplicity.

Men, then, are the only means God's Spirit has of accomplishing His purpose. What men? You. Is it worth doing, or is it not? Is it worth while joining Christ's Society, or is it not? What do *you* do all day? What is your personal stake in the coming of the Kingdom of Christ on earth? You are not interested in

religion, you tell me; you do not care for your
"soul." It was not about your religion I
ventured to ask, still less about your soul.
That you have no religion, that you do not
care for your soul, does not absolve you from
caring for the world in which you live. But
you do not believe in this church, you reply,
or accept this doctrine, or that. Christ does
not, in the first instance, ask your thoughts,
but your work. No man has a right to postpone
his *life* for the sake of his thoughts. Why?
Because this is a real world, not a *think*
world. Treat it as a real world—act. Think
by all means, but think also of what is actual,
of what like the stern world is, of how much
even you, creedless and churchless, could do
to make it better. The thing to be anxious
about is not to be right with man, but with
mankind. And, so far as I know, there is
nothing so on all fours with mankind as
Christianity.

There are versions of Christianity, it is true,
which no self-respecting mind can do other
than disown—versions so hard, so narrow, so
unreal, so super-theological, that practical
men can find in them neither outlet for their
lives nor resting-place for their thoughts.

With these we have nothing to do. With these Christ had nothing to do—except to oppose them with every word and act of His life. It too seldom occurs to those who repudiate Christianity because of its narrowness or its unpracticalness, its sanctimoniousness or its dulness, that these were the very things which Christ strove against and unweariedly condemned. It was the one risk of His religion being given to the common people—an inevitable risk which He took without reserve—that its infinite lustre should be tarnished in the fingering of the crowd or have its great truths narrowed into mean and unworthy moulds as they passed from lip to lip. But though the crowd is the object of Christianity, it is not its custodian. Deal with the Founder of this great Commonwealth Himself. Any man of honest purpose who will take the trouble to inquire at first hand what Christianity really is, will find it a thing he cannot get away from. Without either argument or pressure by the mere practicalness of its aims and the pathos of its compassions, it forces its august claim upon every serious life.

He who joins this Society finds himself in a large place. The Kingdom of God is a Society of the best men, working for the best ends, according to the best methods. Its membership is a multitude whom no man can number; its methods are as various as human nature; its field is the world. It is a Commonwealth, yet it honours a King; it is a Social Brotherhood, but it acknowledges the Fatherhood of God. Though not a Philosophy the world turns to it for light; though not Political it is the incubator of all great laws. It is more human than the State, for it deals with deeper needs; more Catholic than the Church, for it includes whom the Church rejects. It is a Propaganda yet it works not by agitation but by ideals. It is a Religion, yet it holds the worship of God to be mainly the service of man. Though not a Scientific Society its watchword is Evolution; though not an Ethic it possesses the Sermon on the Mount. This mysterious Society owns no wealth but distributes fortunes. It has no minutes for history keeps them; no member's roll for no one could make it. Its entry-money is nothing; its subscription, all you have. The Society never meets and it never adjourns. Its law is one word—loyalty; its Gospel one message—love. Verily "Whosoever will lose his life for My sake shall find it."

The Programme for the other life is not out yet. For this world, for these faculties, for his one short life, I know nothing that is offered to man to compare with membership in the Kingdom of God. Among the mysteries which compass the world beyond, none is greater than how there can be in store for a man a work more wonderful, a life more God-like than this. If you know anything better, live for it; if not, in the name of God and of Humanity, carry out Christ's plan.

PAX VOBISCUM

*Come unto Me all ye that are weary and heavy-laden
And I will give you Rest.
Take My Yoke upon you and learn of Me, for I am
Meek and Lowly in heart, and ye shall find Rest
unto your souls. For my Yoke is easy and My
Burden light.*

PAX VOBISCUM

Introductory

I HEARD the other morning a sermon by a distinguished preacher upon "Rest." It was full of delightful thoughts; but when I came to ask myself, "How does he say I can get Rest?" there was no answer. The sermon was sincerely meant to be practical, yet it contained no experience that seemed to me to be tangible, nor any advice which could help me to find the thing itself as I went about the world that afternoon. Yet this omission of the only important problem was not the fault of the preacher. The whole popular religion is in the twilight here. And when pressed for really working specifics for the experiences with which it deals, it falters, and seems to lose itself in mist.

This want of connection between the great words of religion and every-day life has bewildered and discouraged all of us. Christianity possesses the noblest words in the language; its literature overflows with terms expressive of the greatest and happiest moods which can fill the soul of man. Rest, Joy, Peace, Faith, Love, Light—these words occur with such persistency in hymns and prayers that an observer might think they formed the staple of Christian experience. But on coming to close quarters with the actual life of most of us, how surely would he be disenchanted. I do not think we ourselves are aware how much our religious life is made up of phrases; how much of what we call Christian experience is only a dialect of the Churches, a mere religious phraseology with almost nothing behind it in what we really feel and know.

To some of us, indeed, the Christian experiences seem further away than when we took the first steps in the Christian life. That life has not opened out as we had hoped; we do not regret our religion, but we are disappointed with it. There are times, perhaps, when wandering notes from a diviner music stray into our spirits; but these experiences come at few and fitful moments. We have no sense of possession in them. When they visit us, it is a surprise. When they leave us, it is without explanation. When we wish their return, we do not know how to secure it.

All which points to a religion without solid base, and a poor and flickering life. It means a great bankruptcy in those experiences which give Christianity its personal solace and make it attractive to the world, and a great uncertainty as to any remedy. It is as if we knew everything about health—except the way to get it.

I am quite sure that the difficulty does not lie in the fact that men are not in earnest. This is simply not the fact. All around us Christians are wearing themselves out in trying to be better. The amount of spiritual longing in the world—in the hearts of unnumbered thousands of men and women in whom we should never suspect it; among the wise and thoughtful; among the young and gay, who seldom assuage and never betray their thirst— this is one of the most wonderful and touching facts of life. It is not more heat that is needed, but more light; not more force, but a wiser direction to be given to very real energies already there.

What Christian experience wants is *thread*, a vertebral column, method. It is impossible to believe that there is no remedy for its unevenness and dishevelment, or that the remedy is a secret. The idea, also, that some few men, by happy chance or happier temperament, have acquired the secret—as if there were some sort of knack or trick of it—is wholly incredible. Religion must ripen its fruit for men of every temperament; and the way even into its highest heights must be by a gateway through which the peoples of the world may pass.

I shall try to lead up to this gateway by a very familiar path. But as that path is strangely unfrequented, and even unknown where it passes into the religious sphere, I must dwell for a moment on the commonest of commonplaces.

Nothing that happens in the world happens by chance. God is a God of order. Everything is arranged upon definite principles, and never at random. The world, even the religious world, is governed by law. Character is governed by law. Happiness is governed by law. The Christian experiences are governed by law. Men, forgetting this, expect Rest, Joy, Peace, Faith, to drop into their souls from the air like snow or rain. But in point of fact they do not do so; and if they did they would no less have their origin in previous activities and be controlled by natural laws. Rain and snow do drop from the air, but not without a long previous history. They are the mature effects of former causes. Equally so are Rest, and Peace, and Joy. They, too, have each a previous history. Storms and winds and calms are not accidents, but are brought about by antecedent circumstances. Rest and Peace are but calms in man's inward nature, and arise through causes as definite and as inevitable.

Realise it thoroughly: it is a methodical

not an accidental world. If a housewife turns out a good cake, it is the result of a sound receipt, carefully applied. She cannot mix the assigned ingredients and fire them for the appropriate time without producing the result. It is not she who has made the cake; it is nature. She brings related things together; sets causes at work; these causes bring about the result. She is not a creator, but an intermediary. She does not expect random causes to produce specific effects—random ingredients would only produce random cakes. So it is in the making of Christian experiences. Certain lines are followed; certain effects are the result. These effects cannot but be the result. But the result can never take place without the previous cause. To expect results without antecedents is to expect cakes without ingredients. That impossibility is precisely the almost universal expectation. Now what I mainly wish to do is to help you to firmly grasp this simple principle of Cause and Effect in the spiritual world. And instead of applying the principle generally to each of the Christian experiences in turn, I shall examine its application to one in some little detail. The one I shall select is Rest. And I think anyone who follows the application in this single instance will be able to apply it for himself to all the others.

Take such a sentence as this: African explorers are subject to fevers which cause restlessness and delirium. Note the expression, "cause restlessness." *Restlessness has a cause.* Clearly, then, anyone who wished to get rid of restlessness would proceed at once to deal with the cause. If that were not removed, a doctor might prescribe a hundred things, and all might be taken in turn, without producing the least effect. Things are so arranged in the original planning of the world that certain effects must follow certain causes, and certain causes must be abolished before certain effects can be removed. Certain parts of Africa are inseparably linked with the physical experience called fever; this fever is in turn infallibly linked with a mental experience called restlessness and delirium. To abolish the mental experience the radical method would be to abolish the physical experience, and the way of abolishing the physical experience would be to abolish Africa, or to cease to go there. Now this holds good for all other forms of Restlessness. Every other form and kind of Restlessness in the world has a definite cause, and the particular kind of Restlessness can only be removed by removing the allotted cause.

All this is also true of Rest. Restlessness has a cause: Must not *Rest* have a cause? Necessarily. If it were a chance world we would not expect this; but, being a methodical world, it cannot be otherwise. Rest, physical rest, moral rest, spiritual rest, every kind of rest has a cause, as certainly as restlessness. Now causes are discriminating. There is one kind of cause for every particular effect, and no other; and if one particular effect is desired, the corresponding cause must be set in motion. It is no use proposing finely devised schemes, or going through general pious exercises in the hope that somehow Rest will come. The Christian life is not casual but causal. All nature is a standing protest against the absurdity of expecting to secure spiritual effects, or any effects, without the employment of appropriate causes. The Great Teacher dealt what ought to have been the final blow to this infinite irrelevancy by a single question, "Do men gather grapes of thorns or figs of thistles?"

Why, then, did the Great Teacher not educate His followers fully? Why did He not tell us, for example, how such a thing as Rest might be obtained? The answer is, that *He did*. But plainly, explicitly, in so many words? Yes, plainly, explicitly, in so many words. He assigned Rest to its cause, in words with which each of us has been familiar from our earliest childhood.

He begins, you remember—for you at once know the passage I refer to—almost as if Rest could be had without any cause: "Come unto Me," He says, "and I will *give* you Rest."

Rest apparently was a favour to be bestowed; men had but to come to Him; He would give it to every applicant. But the next sentence takes that all back. The qualification, indeed, is added instantaneously. For what the first sentence seemed to give was next thing to an impossibility. For how, in a literal sense, can Rest be *given*? One could no more give away Rest than he could give away Laughter. We speak of "causing" laughter, which we can do; but we cannot give it away. When we speak of giving pain, we know perfectly well we cannot give pain away. And when we aim at giving pleasure, all that we do is to arrange a set of circumstances in such a way as that these shall cause pleasure. Of course there is a sense, and a very wonderful sense, in which a Great

Personality breathes upon all who come within its influence an abiding peace and trust. Men can be to other men as the shadow of a great rock in a thirsty land. Much more Christ; much more Christ as Perfect Man; much more still as Saviour of the world. But it is not this of which I speak. When Christ said He would give men Rest, He meant simply that He would put them in the way of it. By no act of conveyance would, or could, He make over His own Rest to them. He could give them His receipt for it. That was all. But He would not make it for them; for one thing, it was not in His plan to make it for them; for another thing, men were not so planned that it could be made for them; and for yet another thing, it was a thousand times better that they should make it for themselves.

That this is the meaning becomes obvious from the wording of the second sentence: "Learn of Me and ye shall *find* Rest." Rest, that is to say, is not a thing that can be given, but a thing to be *acquired*. It comes not by an act, but by a process. It is not to be found in a happy hour, as one finds a treasure; but slowly, as one finds knowledge. It could indeed be no more found in a moment than could knowledge. A soil has to be prepared for it. Like a fine fruit, it will grow in one climate and not in another; at one altitude and not at another. Like all growths it will have an orderly development and mature by slow degrees.

The nature of this slow process Christ clearly defines when He says we are to achieve Rest by *learning*. "Learn of Me," He says, "and ye shall find rest to your souls." Now consider the extraordinary originality of this utterance. How novel the connection between these two words, "Learn" and "Rest"? How few of us have ever associated them—ever thought that Rest was a thing to be learned; ever laid ourselves out for it as we would to learn a language; ever practised it as we would practise the violin. Does it not show how entirely new Christ's teaching still is to the world, that so old and threadbare an aphorism should still be so little applied? The last thing most of us would have thought of would have been to associate *Rest* with *Work*.

What must one work at? What is that which if duly learned will find the soul of man in Rest? Christ answers without the least hesitation. He specifies two things—Meekness and Lowliness. "Learn of Me," He says, "for I am *meek* and *lowly* in heart." Now these two things are not chosen at random. To these accomplishments, in a special way, Rest is attached. Learn these, in short, and you have already found Rest. These as they stand are direct causes of Rest; will produce it at once; cannot but produce it at once. And if you think for a single moment, you will see how this is necessarily so, for causes are never arbitrary, and the connection between antecedent and consequent here and everywhere lies deep in the nature of things.

What is the connection then? I answer by a further question. What are the chief causes of *Unrest*? If you know yourself, you will answer Pride, Selfishness, Ambition. As you look back upon the past years of your life, is it not true that its unhappiness has chiefly come from the succession of personal mortifications and almost trivial disappointments which the intercourse of life has brought you? Great trials come at lengthened intervals, and we rise to breast them; but it is the petty friction of our everyday life with one another, the jar of business or of work, the discord of the domestic circle, the collapse of our ambition, the crossing of our will, the taking down of our conceit, which make inward peace impossible. Wounded vanity, then, disappointed hopes, unsatisfied selfishness—these are the old, vulgar, universal sources of man's unrest.

Now it is obvious why Christ pointed out as the two chief objects for attainment the exact opposites of these. To Meekness and Lowliness these things simply do not exist. They cure unrest by making it impossible. These remedies do not trifle with surface symptoms; they strike at once at removing causes. The ceaseless chagrin of a self-centred life can be removed at once by learning Meekness and Lowliness of heart. He who learns them is for ever proof against it. He lives henceforth a charmed life. Christianity is a fine inoculation, a transfusion of healthy blood into an anæmic or poisoned soul. No fever can attack a perfectly sound body; no fever of unrest can disturb a soul which has breathed the air or learned the ways of Christ. Men sigh for the wings of a dove that they may fly away and be at Rest. But flying away will not help us. "The Kingdom of God is *within you.*" We aspire to the top to look for Rest; it lies at the bottom. Water rests only when it gets to the lowest place. So do men. Hence, be lowly. The man who has no opinion of himself at all can never be hurt if others do not acknowledge him. Hence, be meek. He who is without expectation cannot fret if nothing comes to him. It is self-evident that these things are so. The lowly man and the meek man are really above all other men, above all other things. They dominate the world because they do not care for it. The miser does not possess gold, gold possesses him. But the meek possess it. "The meek," said Christ, "inherit the earth." They do not buy it; they do not conquer it; but they inherit it.

There are people who go about the world looking out for slights, and they are necessarily miserable, for they find them at every turn—especially the imaginary ones. One has the same pity for such men as for the very poor. They are the morally illiterate. They have had no real education, for they have never learned how to live. Few men know how to live. We grow up at random, carrying into mature life the merely animal methods and motives which we had as little children. And it does not occur to us that all this must be changed; that much of it must be reversed; that life is the finest of the Fine Arts; that it has to be learned with lifelong patience, and that the years of our pilgrimage are all too short to master it triumphantly.

Yet this is what Christianity is for—to teach men the Art of Life. And its whole curriculum lies in one word—"Learn of Me." Unlike most education, this is almost purely personal; it is not to be had from books or lectures or creeds or doctrines. It is a study from the life. Christ never said much in mere words about the Christian graces. He lived them, He was them. Yet we do not merely copy Him. We learn His art by living with Him, like the old apprentices with their masters.

Now we understand it all? Christ's invitation to the weary and heavy-laden is a call to begin life over again upon a new principle—upon His own principle. "Watch My way of doing things," He says. "Follow Me. Take life as I take it. Be meek and lowly and you will find Rest."

I do not say, remember, that the Christian life to every man, or to any man, can be a bed of roses. No educational process can be this. And perhaps if some men knew how much was involved in the simple "learn" of Christ, they would not enter His school with so irresponsible a heart. For there is not only much to learn, but much to unlearn. Many men never go to this school at all till their disposition is already half ruined and character has taken on its fatal set. To learn arithmetic is difficult at fifty—much more to learn Christianity. To learn simply what it is to be meek and lowly, in the case of one who has had no lessons in that in childhood, may cost him half of what he values most on earth. Do we realise, for instance, that the way of teaching humility is generally by *humiliation*? There is probably no other school for it. When a man enters himself as a pupil in such a school it means a very great thing. There is much Rest there, but there is also much work.

I should be wrong, even though my theme is the brighter side, to ignore the cross and minimise the cost. Only it gives to the cross a more definite meaning, and a rarer value, to connect it thus directly and *causally* with the growth of the inner life. Our platitudes on the "benefits of affliction" are usually about as vague as our theories of Christian Experience. "Somehow," we believe affliction does us good. But it is not a question of "Somehow." The result is definite, calculable, necessary. It is under the strictest law of cause and effect. The

first effect of losing one's fortune, for instance,
is humiliation; and the effect of humiliation,
as we have just seen, is to make one humble;
and the effect of being humble is to produce
Rest. It is a round-about way, apparently, of
producing Rest; but Nature generally works
by circular processes; and it is not certain
that there is any other way of becoming
humble or of finding Rest. If a man could
make himself humble to order, it might
simplify matters, but we do not find that this
happens. Hence we must all go through the
mill. Hence death, death to the lower self
is the nearest gate, and the quickest road to
life.

Yet this is only half the truth. Christ's life
outwardly was one of the most troubled lives
that was ever lived: Tempest and tumult,
tumult and tempest, the waves breaking over
it all the time till the worn body was laid in
the grave. But the inner life was a sea of glass.
The great calm was always there. At any
moment you might have gone to Him and
found Rest. And even when the bloodhounds
were dogging Him in the Streets of Jerusalem
He turned to His disciples and offered them, as
a last legacy, "My peace." Nothing ever for a

moment broke the serenity of Christ's life on earth. Misfortune could not reach him; He had no fortune. Food, raiment, money— fountain-heads of half the world's weariness— He simply did not care for; they played no part in His life; He "took no thought" for them. It was impossible to affect Him by lowering His reputation; He had already made Himself of no reputation. He was dumb before insult. When He was reviled He reviled not again. In fact, there was nothing that the world could do to Him that could ruffle the surface of His spirit.

Such living, as mere living, is altogether unique. It is only when we see what it was in Him that we can know what the word Rest means. It lies not in emotions, nor in the absence of emotions. It is not a hallowed feeling that comes over us in church. It is not something that the preacher has in his voice. It is not in nature, nor in poetry, nor in music —though in all these there is soothing. It is the mind at leisure from itself. It is the perfect poise of the soul; the absolute adjustment of the inward man to the stress of all outward things; the preparedness against every emergency; the stability of assured convictions; the eternal calm of an invulnerable faith; the repose of a heart set deep in God. It is the mood of the man who says, with Browning, "God's in His Heaven, all's well with the world."

Two painters each painted a picture to illustrate his conception of rest. The first chose for his scene a still, lone lake among the far-off mountains. The second threw on his canvas a thundering waterfall, with a fragile birch-tree bending over the foam; at the fork of a branch, almost wet with the cataract's spray, a robin sat on its nest. The first was only *Stagnation*; the last was *Rest*. For in Rest there are always two elements—tranquillity and energy; silence and turbulence; creation and destruction; fearlessness and fearfulness. This it was in Christ.

It is quite plain from all this that whatever else He claimed to be or to do, He at least knew how to live. All this is the perfection of living, of living in the mere sense of passing through the world in the best way. Hence His anxiety to communicate His idea of life to others. He came, He said, to give men life, true life, a more abundant life than they were living; "the life," as the fine phrase in the Revised Version has it "that is life indeed." This is

what He himself possessed, and it was this
which He offers to all mankind. And hence His
direct appeal for all to come to Him who had
not made much of life, who were weary and
heavy laden. These He would teach His secret.
They, also, should know "the life that is life
indeed."

What Yokes are for

There is still one doubt to clear up. After the statement, "Learn of Me," Christ throws in the disconcerting qualification, "*Take My yoke* upon you and learn of Me." Why, if all this be true, does He call it a *yoke*? Why, while professing to give Rest, does He with the next breath whisper "*burden*"? Is the Christian life after all, what its enemies take it for—an additional weight to the already great woe of life, some extra punctiliousness about duty, some painful devotion to observances, some heavy restriction and trammelling of all that is joyous and free in the world? Is life not hard and sorrowful enough without being fettered with yet another yoke?

It is astounding how so glaring a misunderstanding of this plain sentence should ever have passed into currency. Did you ever stop to ask what a yoke is really for? Is it to be a burden to the animal which wears it? It is just the opposite. It is to make its burden light. Attached to the oxen in any other way than by a yoke, the plough would be intoler-

able. Worked by means of a yoke, it is light.
A yoke is not an instrument of torture; it is an
instrument of mercy. It is not a malicious
contrivance for making work hard; it is a
gentle device to make hard labour light. It is
not meant to give pain, but to save pain. And
yet men speak of the yoke of Christ as if it
were a slavery, and look upon those who wear
it as objects of compassion ! For generations
we have had homilies on "The Yoke of Christ,"
some delighting in portraying its narrow
exactions; some seeking in these exactions the
marks of its divinity; others apologising for
it and toning it down; still others assuring us
that, although it be very bad, it is not to be
compared with the positive blessings of
Christianity. How many, especially among the
young, has this one mistaken phrase driven
for ever away from the Kingdom of God?
Instead of making Christ attractive, it makes
Him out a task-master, narrowing life by petty
restrictions, calling for self-denial where none
is necessary, making misery a virtue under
the plea that it is the yoke of Christ, and
happiness criminal because it now and then
evades it. According to this conception,
Christians are at best the victims of a depressing

fate; their life is a penance; and their hope for the next world purchased by a slow martyrdom in this.

The mistake has arisen from taking the word "yoke" here in the same sense as in the expressions "under the yoke" or "wear the yoke in his youth." But in Christ's illustration it is not the *jugum* of the Roman soldier, but the simple "harness" or "ox-collar" of the Eastern peasant. It is the literal wooden yoke which He, with His own hands in the carpenter's shop, had probably often made. He knew the difference between a smooth yoke and a rough one, a bad fit and a good fit; the difference also it made to the patient animal which had to wear it. The rough yoke galled, and the burden was heavy; the smooth yoke caused no pain, and the load was lightly drawn. The badly fitted harness was a misery; the well fitted collar was "easy."

And what was the "burden"? It was not some special burden laid upon the Christian, some unique infliction that he alone must bear. It was what all men bear. It was simply life, human life itself, the general burden of life which all must carry with them from the cradle to the grave. Christ saw that men took life painfully. To some it was a weariness, to others a failure, to many a tragedy, to all a struggle and a pain. How to carry this burden of life had been the whole world's problem. It is still the whole world's problem. And here is Christ's solution: "Carry it as I do. Take life as I take it. Look at it from My point of view. Interpret it upon My principles. Take My yoke and learn of Me, and you will find it easy. For My yoke is easy, works easily, sits right upon the shoulders, and *therefore* My burden is light."

There is no suggestion here that religion will absolve any man from bearing burdens. That would be to absolve him from living, since it is life itself that is the burden. What Christianity does propose is to make it tolerable. Christ's yoke is simply His secret for the alleviation of Human life, His prescription for the best and happiest method of living. Men harness themselves to the work and stress of the world in clumsy and unnatural ways. The harness they put on is antiquated. A rough, ill-fitted collar at the best, they make its strain and friction past enduring, by placing it where the neck is most sensitive; and by mere continuous irritation this sensitiveness increases until the whole nature is quick and sore.

This is the origin, among other things, of a disease called "touchiness"—a disease which, in spite of its innocent name, is one of the gravest sources of restlessness in the world. Touchiness, when it becomes chronic, is a morbid condition of the inward disposition. It is self-love inflamed to the acute point; conceit, *with a hair-trigger*. The cure is to shift the yoke to some other place; to let men and things touch us through some new and perhaps as yet unused part of our nature; to become meek and lowly in heart while the old nature is becoming numb from want of use. It is the beautiful work of Christianity everywhere to adjust the burden of life to those who bear it, and them to it. It has a perfectly miraculous gift of healing. Without doing any violence to human nature it sets it right with life, harmonising it with all surrounding things, and restoring those who are jaded with the fatigue and dust of the world to a new grace of living. In the mere matter of altering the perspective of life and changing the proportions of things, its function in lightening the care of man is altogether its own. The weight of a load depends upon the attraction of the earth. But suppose the attraction of the earth were removed? A ton on some other planet, where the attraction of gravity is less, does not weigh half a ton. Now Christianity removes the attraction of the earth, and this is one way in which it diminishes men's burden. It makes them citizens of another world. What was a ton yesterday is not half a ton to-day. So, without changing one's circumstances, merely by offering a wider horizon and a different standard, it alters the whole aspect of the world.

Christianity as Christ taught it is the truest philosophy of life ever spoken. But let us be quite sure when we speak of Christianity that we mean Christ's Christianity. Other versions are either caricatures, or exaggerations, or misunderstandings, or short-sighted and surface readings. For the most part their attainment is hopeless and the results wretched. But I care not who the person is, or through what vale of tears he has passed, or is about to pass, there is a new life for him along this path.

Were Rest my subject, there are other things I should wish to say about it, and other kinds of Rest of which I should like to speak. But that is not my subject. My theme is that the Christian experiences are not the work of magic but come under the law of Cause and Effect. And I have chosen Rest only as a single illustation of the working of that principle. If there were time I might next run over all the Christian experiences in turn, and show how the same wide law applies to each. But I think it may serve the better purpose if I leave this further exercise to yourselves. I know no Bible study that you will find more full of fruit, or which will take you nearer to the ways of God, or make the Christian life itself more solid or more sure. I shall add only a single other illustration of what I mean, before I close.

Where does Joy come from? I knew a Sunday scholar whose conception of Joy was that it was a thing made in lumps and kept somewhere in Heaven, and that when people

prayed for it, pieces were somehow let down
and fitted into their souls. I am not sure that
views as gross and material are not often held
by people who ought to be wiser. In reality,
Joy is as much a matter of Cause and Effect as
pain. No one can get Joy by merely asking for
it. It is one of the ripest fruits of the Christian
life, and, like all fruits, must be grown. There
is a very clever trick in India called the mango-
trick. A seed is put in the ground and covered
up, and after divers incantations a full-blown
mango-bush appears within five minutes. I
never met anyone who knew how the thing was
done, but I never met anyone who believed it to
be anything else than a conjuring trick. The
world is pretty unanimous now in its belief in
the orderliness of Nature. Men may not know
how fruits grow, but they do know that they
cannot grow in five minutes. Some lives have
not even a stalk on which fruits could hang,
even if they did grow in five minutes. Some
have never planted one sound seed of Joy in all
their lives; and others who may have planted
a germ or two have lived so little in sunshine
that they never could come to maturity.

Whence, then, is Joy? Christ put His teaching
upon this subject into one of the most exquisite

of His parables. I should in any instance have appealed to His teaching here, as in the case of Rest, for I do not wish you to think I am speaking words of my own. But it so happens that He has dealt with it in a passage of unusual fulness.

I need not recall the whole illustration. It is the parable of the Vine. Did you ever think why Christ spoke that parable? He did not merely throw it into space as a fine illustration of general truths. It was not simply a statement of the mystical union, and the doctrine of an indwelling Christ. It was that; but it was more. After He had said it, He did what was not an unusual thing when He was teaching His greatest lessons. He turned to the disciples and said He would tell them why He had spoken it. It was to tell them how to get Joy. "These things I have spoken unto you," He said, "that My joy might remain in you and that your Joy might be full." It was a purposed and deliberate communication of His secret of Happiness.

Go back over these verses, then, and you will find the Causes of this Effect, the spring, and the only spring, out of which true Happiness comes. I am not going to analyse them in

detail. I ask you to enter into the words for
yourselves. Remember, in the first place, that
the Vine was the Eastern symbol of Joy. It was
its fruit that made glad the heart of man. Yet,
however innocent that gladness—for the expressed juice of the grape was the common
drink of every peasant's board—the gladness
was only a gross and passing thing. This was
not true happiness, and the vine of the Palestine
vineyards was not the true vine. *Christ* was
"the *true* Vine." Here, then, is the ultimate
source of Joy. Through whatever media it
reaches us, all true Joy and Gladness find their
source in Christ. By this, of course, is not meant
that the actual Joy experienced is transferred
from Christ's nature, or is something passed
on from Him to us. What is passed on is His
method of getting it. There is, indeed, a sense
in which we can share another's joy or another's
sorrow. But that is another matter. Christ is
the source of Joy to men in the sense in which
He is the source of rest. His people share His
life, and therefore share its consequences, and
one of these is Joy. His method of living is one
that in the nature of things produces Joy. When
He spoke of His Joy remaining with us He
meant in part that the causes which produced it

should continue to act. His followers, that is to say, by *repeating* His life would experience its accompaniments. His Joy, His kind of Joy, would remain with them.

The medium through which this Joy comes is next explained: "He that abideth in Me the same bringeth forth much fruit." Fruit first, Joy next; the one the cause or medium of the other. Fruit-bearing is the necessary antecedent; Joy both the necessary consequent and the necessary accompaniment. It lies partly in the bearing fruit, partly in the fellowship which makes that possible. Partly, that is to say, Joy lies in mere constant living in Christ's presence, with all that that implies of peace, of shelter, and of love; partly in the influence of that Life upon mind and character and will; and partly in the inspiration to live and work for others, with all that that brings of self-riddance and Joy in other's gain. All these, in different ways and at different times, are sources of pure Happiness. Even the simplest of them—to do good to other people—is an instant and infallible specific. There is no mystery about Happiness whatever. Put in the right ingredients and it must come out. He that abideth in Him will bring forth much fruit:

and bringing forth much fruit is Happiness.
The infallible receipt for Happiness, then, is
to do good; and the infallible receipt for doing
good is to abide in Christ. The surest proof
that all this is a plain matter of Cause and
Effect is that men may try every other con-
ceivable way of finding Happiness, and they
will fail. Only the right cause in each case
can produce the right effect.

Then the Christian experiences are our own
making? In the same sense in which grapes are
our own making, and no more. All fruits *grow*
—whether they grow in the soil or in the soul;
whether they are the fruits of the wild grape or
of the True Vine. No man can *make* things
grow. He can *get them to grow* by arranging all
the circumstances and fulfilling all the conditions. But the growing is done by God.
Causes and effects are eternal arrangements,
set in the constitution of the world; fixed
beyond man's ordering. What man can do is
to place himself in the midst of a chain of
sequences. Thus he can get things to grow:
thus he himself can grow. But the grower is
the Spirit of God.

What more need I add but this—test the
method by experiment. Do not imagine that

you have got these things because you know how to get them. As well try to feed upon a cookery book. But I think I can promise that if you try this simple and natural way, you will not fail. Spend the time you have spent in sighing for fruits in fulfilling the conditions of their growth. The fruits will come, must come. We have hitherto paid immense attention to *effects*, to the mere experiences themselves; we have described them, extolled them, advised them, prayed for them—done everything but find out what *caused* them. Henceforth let us deal with causes. "To be," says Lotze, "is to be in relations." About every other method of living the Christian life there is an uncertainty. About every other method of acquiring the Christian experiences there is a "perhaps." But in so far as this method is the way of nature, it cannot fail. Its guarantee is the laws of the universe, and these are "the Hands of the Living God."

THE MAN AFTER GOD'S
OWN HEART

THE MAN AFTER GOD'S
OWN HEART

A Bible Study on the Ideal of a Christian Life

"A man after mine own heart, who shall fulfil
all my will."—ACTS 13. 22

NO MAN can be making much of his life who
has not a very definite conception of what
he is living for. And if you ask, at random, a
dozen men what is the end of their life, you
will be surprised to find how few have formed
to themselves more than the most dim idea.
The question of the *summum bonum* has ever
been the most difficult for the human mind to
grasp. What shall a man do with his life?
What is life for? Why is it given? These have
been the one great puzzle for human books and
human brains; and ancient philosophy and
mediæval learning and modern culture alike
have failed to tell us what these mean.

No man, no book save one, has ever told the
world what it wants; so each has had to face
the problem in his own uncertain light, and

carry out, each for himself, the life that he thinks best.

Here is one who says literature is the great thing—he will be a literary man. He lays down for himself his ideal of a literary life. He surrounds himself with the best ideals of style; and with his great ambition working towards great ends, after great models, he cuts out for himself what he thinks is his great life work. Another says the world is the great thing—he will be a man of the world. A third will be a business man; a fourth, a man of science. And each follows out his aim.

And the Christian must have a definite aim and model for his life. These aims are great aims, but not great enough for him. His one book has taught him a nobler life than all the libraries of the rich and immortal past. He may wish to be a man of business, or a man of science, and indeed he may be both. But he covets a nobler name than these. He will be the man after God's own heart. He has found out the secret philosophy never knew, that the ideal life is this—"A man after Mine own heart, who shall fulfil all My will." And just as the man of the world, or the literary man, lays down a programme for the brief span of his working life, which he feels must vanish shortly in the Unknown of the grave, so much more will the Christian for the great span of his life before it arches over into eternity.

He is a great man who has a great plan for his life—the greatest who has the greatest plan and keeps it. And the Christian should have the greatest plan, as his life is the greatest, as his work is the greatest, as his life and his work will follow him when all this world's is done.

Now we are going to ask to-day, What is the true plan of the Christian life? We shall need a definition that we may know it, a description that we may follow it. And if you look, you will see that both, in a sense, lie on the surface of our text. "A man after Mine own heart"— here is the definition of what we are to be. "Who shall fulfil all My will,"—here is the description of how we are to be it. These words are the definition and the description of the model human life. They describe the man after God's own heart. They give us the key to the Ideal Life.

The general truth of these words is simply this: that the end of life is to do God's will. Now that is a great and surprising revelation. No man ever found that out. It has been before the world these eighteen hundred years, yet few have even found it out to-day. One will tell you the end of life is to be true. Another will tell you it is to deny self. Another will say it is to keep the Ten Commandments. A fourth will point you to the Beatitudes. One will tell you it is to *do* good, another that it is to *get* good, another that it is to *be* good. But the end of life is in none of these things. It is more than all, and it includes them all. The end of life is not to deny self, nor to be true, nor to keep the Ten Commandments—it is simply to do God's will. It is not to get good, nor be good, nor even to do good—it is just what God wills, whether that be working or waiting, or winning, or losing, or suffering, or recovering, or living, or dying.

But this conception is too great for us. It is not practical enough. It is the greatest conception of man that has ever been given to the world. The great philosophers, from Socrates and Plato to Immanuel Kant and Mill, have given us their conception of an ideal human life. But none of them is at all so great as this. Each of them has constructed an ideal human life, a universal life they call it, a life for all other lives, a life for all men and all time to copy. None of them is half so deep, so wonderful, so far-reaching, as this: "A man after Mine own heart, who shall fulfil all My will."

But exactly for this very reason it is at first sight impracticable. We feel helpless beside a truth so great and eternal. God must teach us these things. Like little children, we must sit at His feet and learn. And as we come to Him with our difficulty, we find He has prepared two practical helps for us, that He may humanise the lesson and bring it near to us, so that by studying these helps, and following them with willing and humble hearts, we shall learn to copy into our lives the great ideal of God.

The two helps which God has given us are these:

1. The Model Life realised in Christ, the living Word.

2. The Model Life analysed in the Bible, the written Word.

The usual method is to deal almost exclusively with the first of these. To-day, for certain reasons, we mean to consider the second. As regards the first, of course, if a man could follow Christ he would lead the model life. But what is meant by telling a man to follow

Christ? How is it to be done? It is like putting
a young artist before a Murillo or a Raphael,
and telling him to copy it. But even as the
artist in following his ideal has colours put
into his hand, and brush and canvas, and a hint
here from his master, and a touch there from
another, so with the pupil in the school of
Christ. The great Master Himself is there to
help him. The Holy Spirit is there to help him.
But the model of life is not to be mystically
attained. There is spirituality about it, but no
unreality. So God has provided another great
help, our second help: The Model life analysed
in the Word of God. Without the one, the ideal
life would be incredible; without the other, it
would be unintelligible. Hence God has given
us two sides of this model life: realised in the
Living Word; analysed in the written Word.

Let us search our Bibles then to find this ideal
life, so that copying it in our lives, reproducing
it day by day and point by point, we may learn
to make the most of our life, and have it said of
us, as it was of David, "A man after Mine own
heart, who shall fulfil all My will."

(1) The first thing our ideal man wants is a
reason for his being alive at all. He must
account for his existence. What is he here for?

And the Bible answer is this: "I come to do Thy will, O God" (Heb. 10. 7).

That is what we are here for—to do God's will. "I come to do Thy will, O God." That is the object of your life and mine—to do God's will. It is not to be happy or to be successful, or famous, or to do the best we can, and get on honestly in the world. It is something far higher than this—to do God's will. There, at the very outset, is the great key to life. Anyone of us can tell in a moment whether our lives are right or not. Are we doing God's will? We do not mean, Are we doing God's work? —preaching or teaching, or collecting money —but God's *will*. A man may think he is doing God's work, when he is not even doing God's will. And a man may be doing God's work and God's will quite as much by hewing stones or sweeping streets, as by preaching or praying. So the question just means this—Are we working out our common every-day life on the great lines of God's will? This is different from the world's model life. "I come to push my way." This is the world's idea of it. "Not my way, not my will, but Thine be done"— this is the Christian's. This is what the man after God's own heart says: "I seek not mine own will, but the will of Him that sent me."

(2) The second thing the ideal man needs is
Sustenance. After he has got life, you must give
him food. Now, what food shall you give
him? Shall you feed him with knowledge, or
with riches, or with honour, or with beauty,
or with power, or truth? No; there is a rarer
luxury than these—so rare, that few have ever
more than tasted it; so rich that they who have
will never live on other fare again. It is this:
"My meat is to do the will of Him that sent
Me" (John 4. 34).

Again, to do God's will. That is what a man
lives for: it is also what he lives on. *Meat*.
Meat is strength, support, nourishment. The
strength of the model life is drawn from the
Divine will. Man has a strong will. But
God's will is everlasting strength—Almighty
strength. Such strength the ideal man gets.
He grows by it, he assimilates it—it is his life.
"Man shall not live by bread alone, but by every
word that cometh out of God." Nothing can
satisfy his appetite but this. He hungers to do
God's will. Nothing else will fill him. Every
one knows that the world is hungry. But the
hungry world is starving. It has many meats
and many drinks, but there is no nourishment

in them. It has pleasures, and gaiety, and excitement; but there is no food there for the immortal craving of the soul. It has the theatre and worldly society, and worldly books, and worldly lusts. But these things merely intoxicate. There is no sustenance in them. So our ideal life turns its eye from them all with unutterable loathing. "*My* meat is to do God's will." To do God's will! No possibility of starving on such wonderful fare as this. God's will is eternal. It is eternal food the Christian lives upon. In spring-time it is not sown, and in summer drought it cannot fail. In harvest it is not reaped, yet the storehouse is ever full. Oh, what possibilities of life it opens up! What possibilities of growth! What possibilities of work! How a soul develops on God's will!

(3) The next thing the ideal man needs is *Society*. Man is not made to be alone. He needs friendships. Without society, the ideal man would be a monster, a contradiction. You must give him friendship. Now, whom will you give him? Will you compliment him by calling upon the great men of the earth to come and minister to him? No. The ideal man does not want compliments. He has better food. Will

you invite the ministers and the elders of the
Church to meet him? Will you offer him the
companionship of saint or angel, or seraphim
or cherubim, as he treads his path through the
wilderness of life? No; for none of these will
satisfy him. He has a better friendship than
saint or angel or seraphim or cherubim. The
answer trembles on the lip of every one who is
trying to follow the ideal life: "*Whosoever shall
do the will of My Father which is in Heaven, the
same is My brother, and sister, and mother*" (Matt.
12. 50; Mark 3. 35).

Yes. *My* brother, and *My* sister, and *My*
mother. Mother! The path of life is dark and
cheerless to you. There is a smoother path just
by the side of it—a forbidden path. You have
been tempted many a time to take it. But you
knew it was wrong, and you paused. Then,
with a sigh, you struck along the old weary
path again. It was the will of God, you said.
Brave mother! Oh, if you knew it, there was
a voice at your ear just then, as Jesus saw the
brave thing you had done, "*My* mother!" "He
that doeth the will of My Father, the same is
My mother." Yes; this is the consolation of
Christ—"My mother." What society to be in!
What about the darkness of the path, if we

have the brightness of His smile? Oh! it is
better, as the hymnist says:

> "It is better to walk in the dark with God,
>   Than walk alone in the light;
> It is better to walk with Him by faith,
>   Than walk alone by sight."

Some young man here is suffering fierce
temptation. To-day he feels strong; but
to-morrow his Sabbath resolutions will desert
him. What will his companions say, if he does
not join them? He cannot face them if he is to
play the Christian. Companions! What are
all the companions in the world to this? What
are all the friendships, the truest and the best,
to this dear and sacred brotherhood of Christ?
"He that doeth the will of My Father, the same
is *My* brother."

My mother, my brother, and my sister. He
has a sister—some sister here. Sister! Your
life is a quiet and even round of common and
homely things. You dream, perhaps, of a
wider sphere, and sigh for a great and useful
life, like some women whose names you know.
You question whether it is right that life
should be such a little bundle of very little

things. But nothing is little that is done for
God, and it must be right if it be His will. And
if this common life, with its homely things, is
God's discipline for you, be assured that in
your small corner, your unobserved, un-
ambitious, simple woman's lot is very near
and very dear to Him Who said, "Whosoever
doeth the will of My Father, the same is My
sister."

(4) Now we have found the ideal man a
Friend. But he wants something more. He
wants *Language*. He must speak to his Friend.
He cannot be silent in such company. And
speaking to such a Friend is not mere con-
versation. It has a higher name. It is com-
munion. It is prayer. Well, we listen to hear
the ideal man's prayer. Something about
God's will it must be; for that is what he is
sure to talk about. That is the object of His
life. That is his meat. In that he finds his
society. So he will be sure to talk about it.
Every one knows what his prayer will be.
Every one remembers the words of the ideal
prayer: "*Thy will be done*" (Matt. 6. 10).

Now mark the emphasis on *done*. He prays
that God's will may be done. It is not that
God's will may be borne, endured, put up with.

There is activity in his prayer. It is not mere resignation. How often is this prayer toned off into mere endurance, sufferance, passivity. "Thy will be done," people say resignedly. "There is no help for it. We may just as well submit. God evidently means to have His way. Better to give in at once and make the best of it." Well this is far from the ideal prayer. It may be noble to suffer God's will than to do it; perhaps it is. But there is nothing noble in resignation of this sort—this resignation under protest as it were. And it disguises the meaning of the prayer, "Thy will be done." It is intensely active. It is not an acquiescence simply in God's dealing. It is a cry for more of God's dealing—God's dealing with me, with everything, with everybody, with the whole world. It is an appeal to the mightiest energy in heaven or earth to work, to make more room for itself, to energise. It is a prayer that the Almighty energies of the Divine will may be universally known, and felt, and worshipped.

Now the ideal man has no deeper prayer than that he wants to get into the great current of Will, which flows silently out of Eternity, and swiftly back to Eternity again. His only chance of happiness, of usefulness, of work, is to join

the living rill of his will to that. Other
Christians miss it, or settle on the banks of the
great stream; but he will be among the forces
and energies and powers, 'that he may link
his weakness with God's greatness, and his
simplicity with God's majesty, that he may
become a force, an energy, a power for Duty
and God. Perhaps God may do something
with him. Certainly God will do something in
him—for it is God who worketh in him both to
will and to do of His good pleasure. So his one
concern is to be kept in the will of God.

The ideal man has no deeper prayer than that.
It is the truest language of his heart. He does
not want a bed of roses, or his pathway strewn
with flowers. He wants to do God's will. He
does not want health or wealth, nor does he
covet sickness or poverty,—just what God sends.
He does not want success—even success in
winning souls—or want of success. What
God wills for him, that is all. He does not
want to prosper in business, or to keep barely
struggling on. God knows what is best. He
does not want his friends to live, himself to
live or die. God's will be done. The currents
of his life flow far below the circumstances of
things. There is a deeper principle in it than to

live to gratify himself. And so he simply asks,
that in the ordinary round of his daily life
there may be no desire of his heart more deep,
more vivid, more absorbingly present than this,
" Thy will be done." He who makes this the
prayer of his life will know that of all prayer
it is the most truly blessed, the most nearly in
the spirit of Him who sought not His own will,
but the will of Him that sent Him.

" Lord Jesus, as Thou wilt! if among thorns I go
    Still sometimes here and there let a few roses
        blow.
    No! Thou on earth along the thorny path hast
        gone,
    Then lead me after Thee, my Lord; Thy will
        be done."   *Schmolk.*

(5) But the ideal man does not always pray.
There is such perfect blessedness in praying the
ideal prayer that language fails him sometimes. The peace of God passes all under-
standing, much more all expression. It comes
down upon the soul, and makes it ring with
unutterable joy. And language stops. The ideal
man can no longer pray to his Friend. So his
prayer changes into *Praise.* He is too full to

speak, so his heart bursts into song. Therefore
we must find in the Bible the praise of his lips.
And who does not remember in the Psalms the
song of the ideal man? The huntsmen would
gather at night to sing of their prowess in the
chase, the shepherd would chant the story of
the lion or the bear which he killed as he
watched his flocks. But David takes down his
harp and sings a sweeter psalm than all: "*Thy
Statutes have been my Songs in the House of my
pilgrimage*" (Ps. 119. 54). He knows no
sweeter strain. How different from those who
think God's law is a stern, cold thing! God's
law is His written will. It has no terrors to
the ideal man. He is not afraid to think of its
sternness and majesty. "I will meditate on Thy
laws day and night," he says. He tells us the
subject of his thoughts. Ask him what he is
thinking about at any time. "Thy laws," he
says. How he can please his Master, what more
he can bear for Him, what next he can do for
Him—he has no other pleasure in life than this.
You need not speak to him of the delights of
life. "I will delight myself in Thy statutes," he
says. You see what amusements the ideal man
has. You see where the sources of his enjoyment are. Praise is the overflow of a full heart.

When it is full of enjoyment it overflows; and you can tell the kind of enjoyment from the kind of praise that runs over. The ideal man's praise is of the will of God. He has no other sources of enjoyment. The cup of the world's pleasure has no attraction for him. The delights of life are bitter. Here is his only joy, his only delight: "I delight to do Thy will, O my God" (Ps. 40. 8).

(6) The next thing the ideal man wants is *Education*. He needs teaching. He must take his place with the other disciples at his Master's feet. What does he want from the great Teacher? Teach me Wisdom? No. Wisdom is not enough. Teach me what is Truth? No, not even that. Teach me how to do good, how to love, how to trust? No, there is a deeper want than all. "*Teach me to do Thy will*" (Ps. 143. 10). This is the true education. Teach me to do Thy will. This was the education of Christ. Wisdom is a great study, and truth, and good works, and love, and trust, but there is an earlier lesson—obedience. So the ideal pupil prays, "Teach me to do Thy will."

And now we have almost gone far enough. These are really all the things the ideal man can need. But in case he should want anything else, God has given the man after his own heart a promise. God never leaves anything unprovided for. An emergency might arise in the ideal man's life; or he might make a mistake or lose heart, or be afraid to ask his Friend for some very great thing he needed, thinking it was too much, or for some very little thing, thinking it unworthy of notice. So God has given:

(7) The ideal *Promise*: "If we ask anything according to His will, He heareth us . . . and we know that we have the petitions that we desired from Him" (1 John 5. 14). If he ask anything—no exception—no limit to God's confidence in him. He trusts him to ask right things. He is guiding him, even in what he asks, if he is the man after God's own heart; so God sets no limit to his power. If anyone is doing God's will let him ask anything. It is God's will that he ask anything. Let him put His promise to the test.

Notice here what the true basis of prayer is. The prayer that is answered is the prayer after God's will. And the reason for this is plain. What is God's will is God's wish. And when a man does what God wills, he does what God

wishes done. Therefore God will have that
done at any cost, at any sacrifice. Thousands
of prayers are never answered, simply because
God does not wish them. If we pray for any
one thing, or any number of things we are
sure God wishes, we may be sure our wishes
will be gratified. For our wishes are only the
reflection of God's. And the wish in us is
almost equivalent to the answer. It is the
answer casting its shadow backwards. Already
the thing is done in the mind of God. It casts
two shadows—one backward, one forward.
The backward shadow—that is the wish before
the thing is done, which sheds itself in prayer.
The forward shadow—that is the joy after the
thing is done, which sheds itself in praise.
Oh, what a rich and wonderful life this ideal
life must be! Asking anything, getting everything, willing with God, praying with God,
praising with God. Surely it is too much,
this last promise. How can God trust us with
a power so deep and terrible? Ah, He can trust
the ideal life with anything. "If he ask anything." Well, if he do, he will ask nothing
amiss. It will be God's will if it is asked. It
will be God's will if it is not asked. For he is
come, this man, "*to do God's will.*"

(8) There is only one thing more which the model man may ever wish to have. We can imagine him wondering, as he thinks of the unspeakable beauty of this life—of its angelic purity, of its divine glory, of its Christ-like unselfishness, of its heavenly peace—how long this life can last. It may seem too bright and beautiful, for all things fair have soon to come to an end. And if any cloud could cross the true Christian's sky, it would be when he thought that this ideal life might cease. But God, in the riches of His forethought, has rounded off this corner of his life with a great far-reaching text, which looks above the circumstance of time, and projects his life into the vast eternity beyond. "*He that doeth the will of God abideth for ever*" (1 John 2. 17).

May God grant that you and I may learn to live this great and holy life, remembering the solemn words of Him who lived it first, who only lived it all: "Not every one that saith unto me, Lord, Lord, shall enter into the Kingdom of Heaven; but he that doeth the will of My Father which is in Heaven."